Social Enjoyment Groups
for Children, Teens and
Young Adults with Autism
Spectrum Disorders

Guiding Toward Growth

JOHN MERGES

Jessica Kingsley *Publishers*
London and Philadelphia

Up the River game reproduced with permission from Ravensburger USA, Inc.

First published in 2011
by Jessica Kingsley Publishers
116 Pentonville Road
London N1 9JB, UK
and
400 Market Street, Suite 400
Philadelphia, PA 19106, USA
www.jkp.com

Library of Congress Cataloging in Publication Data
A CIP catalog record for this book is available from the Library of Congress

British Library Cataloguing in Publication Data
A CIP catalogue record for this book is available from the British Library

ISBN 978 1 84905 834 6

Printed and bound in the United States by
Thomson-Shore, 7300 Joy Road, Dexter, MI 48130

To Sharon

The most...

...and forever

Contents

Acknowledgments   7

Part I Introduction and Guiding Principles
1. Beginnings   11
2. Enjoyment – A Skill   18
3. The Band of Regulation   27

Part II The Hurdles
4. Introduction to the Hurdles   35
5. Keeping Things the Same   37
6. Attention Challenges   42
7. Emotional Regulation Problems   46
8. Organization Deficits   51
9. Language Processing Issues   55
10. Associative Thinking   60
11. Sensory Sensitivities   65
12. "Unlearning" Rituals   72
13. Stereotyping by Neurotypical Individuals   77
14. Motivational Deficits   82

Part III FunJoyment Groups
15. Introduction to FunJoyment Groups   89
16. Concepts Important in All Groups   91
17. School-Based Groups for Five-, Six-, and Seven-Year-Old
    Youngsters   99
18. School-Based Groups for Seven- through Eleven-Year-Old
    Youngsters   112
19. School-Based Groups for Junior High and High School Students 121
20. Notes About Community-Based Groups   127
21. Community-Based Groups for Ten- and Eleven-Year-Old
    Youngsters   132
22. Community-Based Groups for Junior High and Senior High
    Students   139
23. Community-Based Groups for Older High Students and Young
    Adults   148

Part IV Materials and Activities

24. Sample Permission Letters   155
25. Scoreboard   160
26. Activities for Five-, Six- and Seven-Year-Olds   161
        Big Dice   161
        Ask to Play   164
        Charades   169
        Ask for Help   170
        Ask to Share   172
        Interrupting a Adult   174
        Bean Bag Toss   176

27. Activities for All Other Groups   178
        A Through Z Game   178
        Apples to Apples   179
        Bean Bag Toss   180
        Bocce Ball   180
        Dominion   181
        First/Last Game   181
        Frisbee Golf   182
        Imaginiff   183
        In a Pickle   183
        Introductory Questions   184
        Killer Bunnies   185
        Kinder Bunnies   186
        Loaded Questions   186
        Mr M's Minefield   187
        Mr M's Uno   189
        Moose in the House   190
        Password   191
        Perudo   192
        Pick It   193
        Pit   195
        Question Cards   195
        Smart Ass   196
        Sort it Out   197
        Tsuro   198
        Turnabout   198
        Twenty Questions   198
        Up the River   199

Index   205

Acknowledgments

There are many people who have influenced my life and my career. I will begin with the professionals.

Early in my career, I was fortunate to be able to work with William Seabloom, Ph.D., L.I.C.S.W., in an innovative program he developed to work with adolescent sex offenders. I learned many things from Bill, but the most important were these two:

1. Never settle for "okay" results – expect outstanding results, and expect the most from each and every client.

2. Open-ended groups allow culture to be transferred, and can thus create increasingly high standards and expectations. Individuals introduced into open-ended groups can quickly learn the culture, and can thus make huge strides quickly.

For the last ten years, Sheila Merzer, M.A., L.P., has helped shape my professional career in private practice. She has guided me to potential clients, and her confidence in me has helped me develop many of the interventions described in this book.

As I began to develop the first social enjoyment experiences in schools, speech/language therapists were incredibly important, helpful, and supportive. In particular, Tahirih Bushey, Diane Arenson, and Sandi Karnowski, all of whom worked with me in the Hopkins School District, played significant roles.

Since beginning private practice, many school districts and charter schools have helped me hone my skills and develop new programming. In particular, Minneapolis, Mounds View, Centennial, and Buffalo School districts have asked me to provide services to multiple groups and individuals. Lionsgate Academy, a charter school, has done the same. I am also grateful to the following schools districts and charter schools (all in Minnesota) for asking me to consult and provide services to their students: Albert Lea, Belle Plaine, Brainerd, Brooklyn Center, Eden Prairie, Forest Lake, Great River Academy,

Inver Grove Heights, Mahtomedi, Montgomery, New Prague, Orono, Owatonna, Redwood Falls, Rockford, St. Paul, Wayzata, and White Bear Lake. Their interest in my work and confidence in my services is much appreciated.

As I began developing the community-based groups, the cooperation of a local non-profit agency, Reach for Resources, was extremely important. The organizations that provide us with terrific spaces – The Depot Coffee House and the Pavilion Community Center (both in Hopkins), and White Bear Lake Community Education services – have contributed to the success of those groups.

The staff working with the community groups – especially Jeff Holmes and Kelly Merges – has led to stable and successful programs. I cannot thank them enough for their dedication and reliability.

Grant Merges provided the outstanding graphics contained in this book.

The time that Sarah Payne and Grant Merges spent visiting groups and taking photos is much appreciated. Their professional work led to two of the photos that grace the cover.

The faith and support of all the parents of the group members has been humbling, inspiring, and vital.

The assistance of Lisa Clark and all the staff at Jessica Kingsley Publishers in making this book possible is very much appreciated.

Finally, my family has been a terrific and constant support as I developed the FunJoyment programming and wrote this book. I have already noted the professional contributions of my adult children, Kelly and Grant, but their interest in the work and faith in me has also been a gift.

Most of all, my wonderful wife, Sharon, has been a guide, and mentor and a best friend. Sharon (who is a professional Life Coach) has the rare, wonder gift of being able to see possibilities in the mists of life, and to clearly but gently guide not only me, but many of her friends and clients, to take risks that lead to personal growth and professional rewards. I am privileged to be able to wake up each day and spend time with her.

Part 1

Introduction and Guiding Principles

Chapter 1

Beginnings

As it is with everything around us, even though we want things to be very linear, to have everything develop in some type of logical sequence, life just happens. Ideas happen along in fits and starts, in brilliant moments when everything becomes startlingly clear, and long months when we can't quite see through the haze of the pressures of daily events.

Guiding Toward Growth was developed over 20 years, but there were many beginnings. Many times when, for a few shining moments, something became wonderfully clear. It was in those moments that either the questions or the answers crystallized. Those moments are chronicled below.

Summer 2006

During the summer of 2006, I made the change that my wife and my friends had been urging me to do. I left the security of working full-time for a local school district and part-time in private practice, to work full-time in private practice with a friend and mentor. The practice focused almost exclusively in assessments, consultations, workshops, and therapy with individuals and families when an autism spectrum disorder (ASD) is present. My shingle was on the door. I was my own boss.

Much of my work came from providing consultation and trainings to school districts, but I wanted to build an office therapy practice as well. As luck would have it, two of my first clients were 30-year-old men referred to me by their parents. Both had the clinical diagnosis of Asperger's syndrome. Both had completed high school and done some college classes. The parents' requests were the same: "Can you help my son become able to get out of the basement of our house? He stays in the basement surfing the web, playing videogames, and trading on eBay all day – and sometimes all night. Can you get him to get involved in the world?"

One of the young men had a job. He worked the overnight shift in a parking garage. He brought a book and a radio to work. He liked the shifts when all he had to do was make change. He worried each night that some customer would want to chat with him or, worse, present a problem that needed to be solved. When I asked him for examples of problems he might be asked to solve, he gave these:

> "Hey buddy, where's a good place to get breakfast at three
> in the morning?"
> "Hey there – how do you get to the airport from here?"

When he was asked a question, it triggered so much anxiety that he usually called in sick for two days. He was seriously considering quitting the job.

The other young man had been employed as a custodian in an office building – again the night shift. He had enjoyed his job for many months, and planned to keep it. It was just his supervisor and himself, and his supervisor was a taciturn man. Work began with a few brief instructions. During lunch and breaks the pair would sit quietly – sometimes reading, sometimes listening to music through earphones – never interacting. My client felt relaxed and calm.

Then the supervisor was transferred. My client got a new supervisor. And this supervisor was gregarious and out-going. He wanted to talk about everything – sports, politics, movies, the weather – basically full-time chatter. The supervisor changed the routine so that the pair always worked together so he could talk non-stop. My client did the only thing he could think of: he quit the job. He had not worked since.

I met with both of these men. I liked them. I enjoyed finding out about them. Together we explored employment and community involvement activities that seemed to suit people who wanted to be productive (and even precise), but wanted to be left alone. I (or maybe we) was not successful. Both stopped coming to see me. Both stayed in their parents' basements. Both most likely are there still.

Some clinicians I have spoken to comment on cases like this to the effect that these young men have not experienced enough pain or stress, and thus they are not yet motivated to change. I thought the opposite. I thought they were both in too much pain and under too much stress to consider doing anything to change their lives. Both men were not enjoying life, and both knew that. They, however, believed any change to their lives would only be for the worse. They lacked the ease and confidence necessary to take on the social interaction challenges of employment. It was a tough moment for me. I knew I did not have the skills to help these men get out of their basements.

I did, however, decide that I wanted to develop a program to keep other young men from going into the basement. A beginning...

Fall 1984

I was beginning my fourth year as a school social worker. My assignment for the year was at an elementary self-contained program for special education students with high levels of need. Some of the children had the medical diagnosis of autism. I had never heard of autism. I was directed to provide weekly social skills programming for these students. I was assigned to do it in groups – doing groups would allow the teachers to send their students to me so they could gain preparation time.

Fortunately, a young gifted speech therapist had also been assigned to the program. She was directed to provide weekly speech groups to the students – another way for the teachers to gain their preparation time. In a moment of genius serendipity, she and I decided to co-lead the groups, and thus meet twice a week. We did this because we enjoyed working together, and also because neither of us knew what we could possibly do with this unusual group of students.

We researched, and found out that we should be doing role-plays. Through observation, we noted that the students did best in situations that had an element of routine to them. We decided to create a social ritual in which we would try out role-plays that would lead the children to use more language skills. In another moment of accidental brilliance, we decided to videotape the sessions.

The videotapes revealed our initial ineptness, but then our developing skills. But they also revealed something unexpected. When our plans fell apart (remember, this was the 1980s and I had grown up watching *Star Trek* on TV), I would look at her, and, using a truly awful Scottish accent, say, "Capt'n, I cannot hold her. She's breakin' up!" We would then together burst into laughter.

The tapes revealed an interesting progression in the students. Initially, they ignored us at these moments. But then they began to look at me when I made the statement, and look at us while we laughed. Over time, they began to smile, and then to laugh. Finally, one or two began to fall off their chairs and roll around while laughing. Sometimes they laughed so hard some of us would begin to tear up. In watching the tapes, she and I realized that we had done something unintended, but wonderful. We had taught the students to enjoy a nonsensical (albeit a ritualistic) moment together. We knew that this was somehow important, but we didn't know why, and we did not realize that anyone else might see any importance in this. But we decided to add more rituals to our groups that ended in laughing and celebration. At times we were accused of having too much fun in the groups and not doing enough teaching. Fortunately, we ignored the criticism. We were on to something. I just didn't know what. A beginning...

May 2002

I had been developing, refining, and creating new role-plays and games for the group concept that the speech therapist and I had created for almost 18 years. I had even begun to identify the groups on IEP[1] documents in a way that distinguished them from the social skills groups that were now proliferating and being published as curriculum. I called the groups Social Interaction/Social Enjoyment.

My education colleagues urged me to go to the state conference of the Autism Society of Minnesota to see and hear Steven Gutstein, Ph.D., talk about his system of intervention called Relationship Development Intervention (RDI). A few who had seen Gutstein or read his book thought that I would like what I would hear. I went and was amazed. Gutstein showed video, and on many of the videos

---

1   For those unfamiliar with the educational system in the United States, an IEP is the Individual Education Plan – the legal document that creates the educational plan for students receiving special education services. It is also used to track progress on that plan.

he interacted in goofy ways that got the clients first smiling and then laughing. He spoke about "enjoying the shared experience", and identified the obstacles to being able to participate in any experience. I bought his book that day. I read it that night, and the next night, and the next. I finally had language that allowed me to articulate what I was attempting to do. I was suddenly much better able to articulate the purpose of the groups. A beginning...

December 2007

Scott[2] was a 20-year-old young man that I had known since he was 17. Scott had stopped going to school. He had stopped leaving his house. He had stopped interacting at all.

Scott probably does not have ASD. He had been assessed many times, and had been given multiple diagnoses – including oppositional defiant disorder, anxiety disorder, attention-deficit hyperactivity disorder, depressive disorder, possible emerging schizophrenia, and adjustment disorder. More than one evaluation had noted that Scott had very slow processing speed, especially auditory processing.

After working with Scott and his parents for six months, I was fortunate in being able to arrange a consult with the clinical social worker who I considered to have the best diagnostic skills of any mental health clinician in the Twin Cities. She listened to my information, reviewed the file, and met with Scott's mom. We decided together that the slow auditory processing speed was the key disability, and that it was causing Scott significant stress: he had great difficulty understanding classroom activities, social relationships, and how to grieve the recent tragic death of his older brother. Although she agreed that Scott did not have ASD, she urged that:

1. The parents and I talk to Scott about his processing disability, and suggested websites to visit that had visual aids that explained brain processing.

2. The parents start using small moments in the day to talk about Scott's brother and how they missed him, and then simply move on until the next small moment.

---

2   Scott's name (and the name of every young person included in this book) has been changed to protect his privacy and the privacy of his family.

3. I utilize the methods that I had developed to help develop social interaction/social enjoyment skills with young people with ASD to help Scott create a link first to me, and then to peers.

We followed the program. Scott slowly began to attend the transition program he was enrolled in. After a year he was attending that school almost full-time. With the support of the transition program, he then began to take a special class at the local technical college. He then joined my young adult weekly social group.

In December 2007, Scott told his mom that she needed to help him go out and buy an expensive set of knives. He had decided to enroll in a culinary arts program at his technical college. I was glad I was sitting in my office (instead of driving) when I received the call from mom telling me about his decision. It would have been very difficult to drive with the film of tears in my eyes. A beginning...

September 2005

I had trained my daughter, Kelly, to co-lead my social interaction/social enjoyment groups. In addition to working for me, Kelly worked for a local non-profit agency which provided social and recreation opportunities for children and adults with cognitive and physical disabilities.

One day Kelly was talking to her supervisor, and the supervisor expressed her frustration with the fact that the agency was now getting so many requests for social opportunities from parents of youths with high-functioning autism and Asperger's syndrome. The agency had been trying to include this type of individual in with their other clients, but the results were very unsatisfactory. The supervisor stated that she wished the agency knew how to create social opportunities specifically for this group. Kelly told her that she and I were doing that exact group experience at a local non-profit coffee house. We had seven participants, but knew there had to be many more possible participants. We had a program, but no way to advertise and enroll the participants. The agency had requests to do a program, sent out mailings outlining their offerings four times a year to hundreds of families and many professionals, had the mechanism to enroll clients, but no program.

Within days a partnership was formed. The only thing we needed was a name. Because she had created the link between the agency and me, I allowed Kelly to name the group. *FunJoyment* was born.[3] A beginning...

FunJoyment continues to be the name of the school and community-based interventions that have been developed using the *Guiding Toward Growth* principles. These interventions will be discussed in detail in Part III of this book.

---

3   The first *FunJoyment* group had seven participants. As of today, I have 55 particpants enrolled in the five groups.

Chapter 2

Enjoyment – A Skill

A few years ago, as I was working on my skills as a consultant to school districts in Minnesota, I was asked by a school district on the fringe of the metropolitan area around the Twin Cities to help them program for a very bright, but very angry, young man with Asperger's syndrome. Karl was about to enter his final year in junior high, but had not been very successful in managing himself when frustrated by peers or by course assignments. He tended to lash out verbally. Because the school administration was just learning about high-functioning students with ASD, they tended to respond with consequences and structure – similar to the way they were responding to students with emotional/behavior disabilities.[1] It was not surprising to me that not only was that approach ineffective, but Karl's behavior was getting more negative, and he had no positive connections with staff or students. Karl went to school every day with a scowl on his face and a chip on his shoulder. Staff "walked on eggshells" around Karl, but, more often than not, problems occurred, Karl was given consequences (up to and including suspensions), and everyone, including Karl's parents, was unhappy.

As part of my work, I spent time hanging out with Karl over the summer. We went out to eat, played games, went to the park to play frisbee golf and take batting practice, and generally laughed a lot. Karl was opinionated and rigid, but I found that creating a schedule for our outings, giving Karl a choice between two things, and providing him with alerts that we were going to transition to another activity or end our time together, revealed a Karl who was both friendly and fun.

---

1   Karl, like many young people with ASD who present with challenging behavior, was first assessed and found eligible for special educations services as a student with an emotional/behavior disability (E/BD).

Near the end of the summer, I scheduled a time to make a tape of an interaction with Karl. The intention was to use the tape to demonstrate Karl's information processing difficulties and quirks, and then capture the way I worked with him to avoid confrontation and frustration. Our plan was then to use the tape to train the school staff with new skills to interact with Karl positively. It was important to avoid falling into the pattern of frustration, negative response, and consequences for this behavior. That would only lead to more frustration in Karl, and set the stage for the whole pattern to repeat.[2]

During the course of the interview, I asked Karl to tell me about his relationships with the other students. His response was so clear and so powerful that it has become a video clip that I use in almost every workshop that I present. Karl talked about how he had become used to being teased and put down, and he now expected kids to treat him that way. But then, he explained, his class had a day-long end-of-the-year "retreat deal thingee" away from school, and lots of kids came right up to him and said, "Karl – I apologize for the way I have treated you, and I won't be treating you like that anymore." Karl talked about how hearing those statements "was like getting hit in the face with a brick". Imagine: Karl had become used to being teased and ostracized, but found that the apology was like a brick in the face. When I asked him to clarify what that meant, Karl explained that he knew how to handle the teasing and the put-downs – what he didn't know how to handle was kids being nice to him. This was because, he explained, if the kids were nice to him, he would have no idea if they really wanted to be friends with him, or if they were setting him up to make fun of him. Since he couldn't gauge the difference between those possibilities, being treated nice would be so stressful that it would be like "getting a brick in the face".

---

2   I often speak about this strategy as "giving the teachers new tools". The analogy is that if a hammer is the only tool you have in your toolbox, it will be the only tool you use when something breaks around the house. If it doesn't seem to be working, you might start to hit things harder, or hit things sideways – often with disastrous results. School staff will often use the hammer (consequences) because it is the only tool they are aware of. When we demonstrate how to use a screwdriver (distracting a student and letting a situation calm down), a wrench (planning ahead to avoid a problem) and pliers (pre-teaching a skill and letting a student practice it while calm), we help school staff stay calm and confident. Because they have more tools, the teachers feel more confident. The student experiences more success, and the staff can praise the student. The situation turns from lose-lose to win-win.

Karl's explanation of what he experiences when he is unable to gauge what neurotypical peers are doing is a core factor in creating the *Guiding Toward Growth* construct for understanding, and then intervention. *Guiding Toward Growth* is based on the development of the skills needed to be at ease in and to enjoy a social situation. And, remember, almost every job has a social component. No matter what the job, people sometimes get together to chat, celebrate birthdays, take up collections when people are dealing with a family illness or death, talk about trials and tribulations, tease, and goof around. When young people with ASD feel awkward with those interactions, they are not likely to seek employment.

Youths with ASD not feeling comfortable enough to seek employment sets up one very large "horizon problem". We are entering a time when many young people with ASD are completing school and becoming old enough to enter the workforce. Although there is not a lot of research into employment for adults with ASD, Cathy Pratt, Board Chair of the Autism Society of America and Director of the Indiana Resource Center for Autism, wrote about this in the first edition of 2007's *Autism Advocate*. That article raises concerns. Sixty-one percent of adults with ASD in Indiana (defined as over 18 years old) were unemployed. Of the remainder, 14 percent were working in sheltered workshops. The remaining 25 percent had typical jobs in their communities. Those employed had an average work-week of 21 hours, and an average income of $6516. To me, that means that most of these young adults would be relying on either governmental assistance or assistance from their families. Even if they are not getting government assistance, they are not paying significant amounts to social security and income taxes to help support the rest of the community needs. With the current rate of identification of infants with ASD at one in every 110 infants, the upcoming horizon problem is huge. If the employability rates and the income levels of these young adults don't rise, there is going to be an increasing cost that families and communities will need to pay in order to support these young people. Would it not be better to help them support themselves, and, in doing so, contribute tax money to help seniors and persons with other disabilities? Would not this direction enhance both their lives and our communities?

More than one autism expert has commented that the main barrier to successful employment for individuals with Asperger's syndrome and high-functioning autism is not academic skills, but lack of understanding and ease in the social world of work. Social enjoyment is a skill. It can be learned.

Now perhaps I am a bit dense, but the realization that social enjoyment is a skill – and, as a skill, something that can be systematically improved upon – was an epiphany moment. Until that moment, my focus on social enjoyment for my young clients was as an area of deficit. Difficulty understanding and being comfortable in the social world was part of the diagnostic criteria – we expected it to be present. We expected it to remain as a part of individuals with ASD for their lifetimes.

But that did not mean that they could not gain skills in this area.

Gradually, I began to view the difficulties that my clients have in understanding and being comfortable in the social world as similar to my difficulties on the golf course. I am not a very good golfer. In fact, my skills are poor – so poor, that for the first 50 years of my life, I tried to stay off golf courses.

As a youth, I played Little League baseball with a lot of success. I played in high school, and eventually made the varsity. I loved playing baseball.

When I did not find success in college, I looked around for other sports in which I could "succeed".[3] I tried golf, and was very frustrated when I would either miss the little white ball, or the flight patterns would be odd and lead directly into trees, sand, ponds, and roadways. When I tried tennis, my baseball skills seemed to translate enough so that I met with what I considered success. I put time, effort and money into tennis and tennis equipment. I also began to run, and eventually entered 5K and 10K races. I measured up to my standard of success in both of these sports.

As I aged, however, my body lost resiliency. Years of throwing curve balls and making tennis serves left me with a damaged rotator cuff. Miles of pounding and three knee operations left my knees vulnerable to pain when I tried to run. My chosen avenues for exercise and fun had become doorways to injury and pain.

---

3   My definition of success: to be able to participate in a sport at a level of skill high enough that I did not feel embarrassed knowing that strangers might be watching me perform.

I decided to give golf a try again.

I took lessons.

I hit buckets of balls.

I learned how to make golf clubs. (Interestingly, I am now a much better golf club maker than golfer. One of my incentives to play golf every spring is to try out the clubs that I made over the winter.)

But I am still a poor golfer.

I had to learn to enjoy playing golf even though I don't play very well. Not playing very well leads me to feel stress and anxiety. I feel this the most on the first tee every time I play. On the first tee, there is often an audience. Other golfers are waiting to tee off. Sometimes there is a restaurant or bar that overlooks the first tee. People watch golfers hit their drive on the first tee, and comment on the shots and on the golfers. First tees filled me with anxiety. I hated first tees. All I could think about on first tees was that everyone must be thinking that I was a terrible golfer.

I had to overcome my anxiety over first tee shots in order to be able to enjoy golf. I did this through:

- Lessons – I hired a golf teacher.

- Practice – I spent lots of money at the driving range. At the driving range you both practice hitting the shot and practice hitting while there are people around who can be watching.

- Embracing the anxiety by making it a part of my life that I was familiar enough with to, if not enjoy, at least not fear.

I decided that if I could master my anxiety of first-tee shots so that I could enjoy a round of golf, my clients ought to be able to improve their social enjoyment skills to the point where they could overcome their anxiety about social interactions at work. I decided that the process had to be the same. I needed to set up situations where my young clients could:

- take lessons

- practice – and practice in a way that included others watching them

- embrace their social anxiety by making it a part of their life that they were familiar enough with to, if not enjoy, at least not fear.

Three decades ago, when I was taking a child development course, I remember studying Piaget. My memory is that Piaget came to his conclusions about children reaching the points where they would move to different levels of sophistication in social interactions by being a passive observer of his own children's development. Somehow I was left with the idea that as children's brains grew, they then reached a certain level of complexity, and the skills needed for more sophisticated social interactions appeared spontaneously. I admit that this may not be what Piaget was saying; it became, however, my construct of how children developed. I have two children, and watching them grow reinforced this notion.

As I thought about social enjoyment as being a set of skills and that those skills can be taught to us by good teachers, I realized my notion was mistaken. Children's brains grow and develop the capacity for greater complexity, but that complexity needs to be learned. I began to observe carefully when I visited preschools, kindergarten classes, and homes with young children, and I revised my thinking. Two major events were happening:

1. children's brains were developing to the point where a relatively complex skill like social enjoyment could be taught, *and*

2. preschool teachers, kindergarten teachers, and parents were systematically pre-teaching, teaching, and reinforcing these skills.

One definition of any ASD is a developmental delay. One way to think about a developmental delay is that it is a delay in the ability of a person's brain to be able to process and incorporate complex learning. My experience working with kindergarten and early-elementary-age ASD students was demonstrating to me not that these children could not learn social enjoyment, but that there was a delay in when they developed the complex neuropathways needed to process and incorporate this learning. In addition, I had been to workshops and been exposed to the new brain-based research that identified that the brains of children with autism were different because of the "too big, too many" phenomenon.[4]

This information created a paradigm shift for me. I realized that I wanted to think about the students as not unable to learn the complex skill of social enjoyment, but delayed in their ability to reach the point where they could learn and incorporate the information, and probably never able to develop it to a high level of proficiency. But I decided that they had the capacity to develop this skill in the same way that I had developed my skill on a golf course. I will never be a good golfer. No one will ever want me on his team in a tournament. But I enjoy being on a golf course. I enjoy the smell of the grass, the beauty of the course, the quiet as I walk to my ball. And once or twice a round, I hit a very sweet shot.

Young people with ASD might never become social butterflies. They may never be comfortable at a cocktail party. But they could learn to enjoy navigating through the social world of work while they are being productive and independent. And, once in a while, they will "hit a sweet shot", enjoy that moment, and gain motivation to move on in anticipation of the next sweet shot.

The huge problem is that because of their delay, when their brains reach the point where they can begin to learn these skills, they have moved beyond the situations (preschool classes and kindergarten) where these skills are systematically being taught. Once they are at the point where they are ready to learn, they are grouped:

- at school with students who are learning much more sophisticated social interaction skills

- with students who can learn these skills at a faster pace

- in settings where multiple kinds of simultaneous learning (e.g. learning academic content and cooperative group skills) are expected.

---

4   This information is based on the presentation made in May 2006 by Margaret L. Bauman, MD, and Thomas L. Kemper, MD, at the annual conference of the Autism Society of Minnesota. The "too big, too many" phenomenon is the discovery that the brains of children with autism at two years old have brain cells that are larger than those of typical children, and that they have many more brain cells. This results in crowding, and the crowding creates problems in the creation of neuropathways.

Think about learning as a series of learning steps. It could be depicted this way:

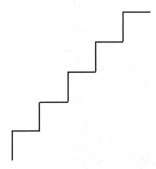

For students with ASD, think about the need to break each step into smaller steps:

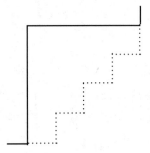

Now think about the probability that each step might take these students more time to master:

It is easy to see that a classroom teacher (especially with the demands of the current local and federal legislation) does not have time to do this in a typical classroom. But it needs to be done.

Guiding Toward Growth interventions do exactly that. *Guiding Toward Growth* breaks skills down into small, recognizable, clear components, and gives students additional time to master each step. With mastery comes the ease and confidence needed to begin to use the skills outside of the group setting.

Chapter 3

The Band of Regulation

All of us need to be ready to learn something that we are being taught. Part of being ready to learn is having our mind, body, and spirit in a relatively calm state. I call this being regulated. All of us have a state of regulation in which we are able to take in information, analyze it, process it, store it, and link it to other learning. All of us, however, have times when we are so "unregulated" that learning is difficult. There are times when we have moved out of our state of regulation and have difficulty learning (or are unable to learn) because we are too upset, too stressed, too preoccupied, too hungry, too wired, and so on. There are also times when we can't quite rouse ourselves enough to get into our *band of regulation* in order to learn, because we are too tired, too bored, too uninterested.

One way to think about this is to create a visual band of regulation:

Over-stimulated
Too much stress/too much anxiety/too much sensory input

Relatively regulated
Ready to learn/ready to work

Under-aroused
Tired, bored, inattentive

As adults, we might not think about this as our band of regulation, but we are all aware of what we need in order to be able to operate more or less efficiently. We try to eat and sleep well. We use breaks in our days to rest. We use exercise and, perhaps, meditation or yoga in order to stay focused and centered. We take days off and vacations in order to recharge our batteries. We drink coffee, energy drinks, or snacks to give ourselves a boost. We use friends and family members as listeners and advisors when we are struggling with difficult issues. We have spent our lives (some of us better than others) figuring out ways to stretch our band of regulation as wide as possible, and have developed ways to help get ourselves back into the band when we are slipping out of it. One way to think about this is that responsible adults have created a wide band of regulation. They can manage themselves in most challenging situations and environments. Most adults have a very wide band of regulation – they can manage their stresses and the things that lead them to be under-aroused in a way that makes them very functional in most situations. Their band looks something like this:

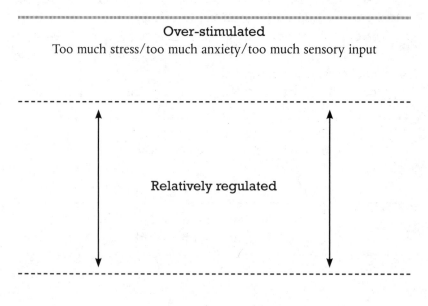

Over-stimulated
Too much stress/too much anxiety/too much sensory input

Relatively regulated

Under-aroused
Tired, bored, inattentive

Children and youths have narrower bands. They benefit, however, by being able to make use of the supports that parents and teachers provide in order to help them stay regulated. Their bands would look something like this:

Over-stimulated
Too much stress/too much anxiety/too much sensory input

Relatively regulated
Able to make use of:
- rewards
- consequences
- warnings
- point systems
- grades
- preparing ahead.

Under-aroused
(When students are young, it is important for the adults to make modifications and accommodations to help students remain in this range. As students get older, we work to help them recognize their state of regulation and begin to advocate for what they need.)

Young people with ASD struggle to remain in the regulated range. Sensory issues, confusion, the pressures to learn and to perform, changes in routine, physical illness, responses to food and drink, the speed at which they can process information, and their ability to process verbal information (as opposed to visual information) make their band relatively narrow:

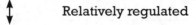

Over-stimulated
Too much stress/too much anxiety/too much sensory input

Relatively regulated

Under-aroused
Tired, bored, inattentive

In addition, they have very little knowledge about what they need in order to remain in a state that is regulated enough so that they might learn.

Guiding Toward Growth interventions are designed in order to:

1. create a predictable and safe setting where it is relatively easy for the young person to stay regulated

2. break social enjoyment skills into small, deliberate steps

3. provide plenty of repetition and practice so that not only can the skills be learned, but also the participants can develop social ease in the situation and confidence in their abilities.

As might be assumed, the level of structure needed to do this varies based on the age and experience of the individuals with ASD. In general, younger individuals and those individuals just being introduced to the group process need more structure and support.

As the *FunJoyment* principles and the structure and content of the groups become familiar to the participants, their band of regulation generally widens, and they need less support.

It is important in the understanding of *Guiding Toward Growth* for the adults to be willing to view any problem that a participant might have in staying regulated as a process problem for the adult leaders to address, not as a character flaw in the participant or as a behavior problem. For example, I once had a kindergarten student who became significantly unregulated when I introduced him to these group principles with even one other classmate. He imitated a wild animal – he growled, bit, and spat at any other child. My solution was to do a *Guiding Toward Growth* group with just the two of us twice per week for seven months. Once he knew, understood, and enjoyed every ritual and activity, I told him that he was going to be my co-leader in the groups and that he and I would lead with three or four of his classmates. Although he initially showed signs of coming out of his band of regulation when we began these groups, he quickly settled and became a conscientious co-leader. More importantly, he had fun, and his classmates, for the first time, had fun interacting with him.

Part II

The Hurdles

Chapter 4

Introduction to the Hurdles

Based on the premise that young people can learn to develop their ability to understand and enjoy social interaction if the skills are taught within a sensible structure, the program would need to:

- make those skills small enough to be learned

- make the skills very clear and teach them very deliberately

- provide more time to learn, master, and become comfortable with each skill

- provide even more time to practice a skill to the point where it can be used with ease and comfort.

However, the program also has to make sure that it addresses the unique hurdles faced by individuals with ASD. Over the course of many years, through gathering information from workshops, trial and error, and careful observation, I have identified specific hurdles that need to be addressed in order to enhance the probability of success in teaching social enjoyment. It is important to note that not every individual runs into the same hurdles, or has the same level of difficulty with each hurdle. Some young people glide past some hurdles and get very stuck trying to navigate past others. But each of the hurdles will present challenges to some individuals, and every individual with ASD will have to deal with many of these hurdles.[1]

---

1   As we go through these hurdles, most readers will recognize one or two that present challenges to their life. The difference for a person with ASD is the number of hurdles faced, and the relative intensity of the challenges.

Persons leading *Guiding Toward Growth* interventions need to be aware of the hurdles, and pre-plan in order to make the paths through and around the hurdles smooth and clear. They should be ready to evaluate problems from the perspective that they result from the young people getting "stuck" trying to navigate through hurdles, rather than the perspective that individuals are making a willful decision to be uncooperative.

The hurdles are:

- Keeping Things the Same/Routine

- Attention Challenges

- Emotional Regulation Problems

- Organization Deficits

- Language Processing Issues

- Associative Thinking

- Sensory Sensitivities

- "Unlearning" Rituals

- Stereotyping by Neurotypical Individuals

- Motivational Deficits.

Part II of this book will guide the reader in understanding each hurdle, and setting the framework for developing effective interventions. Effective interventions allow the young people with ASD to experience enough success to remain motivated to continue working on developing social interaction/social enjoyment skills. The long-term goal is simple: to develop sufficient social interaction/social enjoyment skills that will help these young people maintain themselves within their band of regulation as they enter the complex social environment of post-secondary education and the world of work.

Chapter 5

Keeping Things the Same[1]

None of us likes to feel "out of control". If we think about our lives, we all can identify ways that we structure ourselves so that there is enough "sameness", or routine, to make us comfortable. For example:

- We park our cars in the lots in relatively the same places so that we can easily and comfortably find the cars when we exit the work, shopping, or appointments.

- We hang our clothes in closets and put them into specific dresser drawers in locations that make sense to us and are thus easy to find.

- When we get home, we place our keys, wallets, or purses in specific locations so that we can locate them without thinking when we have to leave.

And, if we are thrown off in our routines – park in a different lot, "lose" an article of clothing because it is hung or placed in the "wrong" location, "lose" our keys because we became distracted and placed them down before we reached our designated "automatic" location – we react with some degree of anxiety or even panic. Some of us react with anger – anger at ourselves or, worse, anger aimed at family members.

It is important to notice in ourselves two realities:

---

1   This hurdle, and every hurdle, tends to be most challenging to the youngest participants, and become less challenging with older participants. In general, more care and planning needs to be placed on this hurdle when working with young children. However, group leaders need to be very aware of this hurdle when they are working with young adults. It may look like something else – oppositional or defiant behavior – but it is important to know that the teen in front of you may be having difficulty with this hurdle.

1. the comfort we experience when our life is moving along in ways that we recognize as routine (and thus, easily within our control)

2. how irritated, angry or even panicked we may become when we face the hurdle of things not going in the way we expected.

Because most of us have been working at building a wide band of regulation and maintaining ourselves within that band, we don't "melt down". However, if we are honest with ourselves, I think we can all describe incidents when we encountered the hurdle of facing circumstances that seemed out of our control.

I faced that circumstance recently while presenting a workshop on the Guiding Toward Growth principles. My presentation includes video clips that help the audience understand the hurdles by actually seeing a young person struggling with particular hurdles.

I have learned that most schools and organizations have LCD projectors that I can use, but many do not have speakers. So, I travel with my own speakers.

On this occasion, I set everything up and was ready to go, but I could get no sound out of my speakers. I tried a few things, and got increasingly panicked when I could not make the speakers work. The program personnel began to look for substitute speakers, but found nothing. My mind was racing and my body was sweating. I could not think of anything else to do.

At that point, one of my associates suggested I shut down the computer, turn off the speakers, unplug everything, and then reattach and turn everything back on. I was literally shaking, so I needed help accomplishing the task. We finished, and it worked. I left the room, took a short walk and many deep breaths, and was able to refocus within my band.

One way of thinking about the rituals and routines of people with ASD is that the rituals help them feel calm and in control. I constantly tell myself that the rituals and routines, no matter how controlling they appear to be, are not the end but the means to the end. The end result is the desire to feel calm and in control.

Young children with ASD demonstrate this quite dramatically. In elementary schools, these students can become quite upset on days when the routine is changed – field trips, fire drills, assemblies, and late-start or early-release days. Our experienced teachers help these students with Social Stories™ [2] and extra support. These are very effective. To my way of thinking, these techniques are ways to teach youngsters new routines that they can then learn to count on. This is similar to the strategy that I have used myself so that I can find my keys every morning – I have taught myself a routine so that the keys end up in the same place every night.

This conceptualization also gives us a way to frame the purpose of a "meltdown" for youngsters. When a child in school melts down, the school usually has developed a plan to help that child. The same people arrive on the scene, the child is taken to a familiar and comfortable location, the location has favorite objects, books, fidgets, weighted blankets, and stuffed animals, and the child begins to calm and get back into his band. We have to be aware that, for some students, the objective of the meltdown may be to get out of a situation that feels out of control, and into a familiar routine that feels very much in control. In other words, the student has become confused, anxious, and/or panicked, and subconsciously takes steps that will eventually result in a soothing, comfortable, routine outcome.

When using Guiding Toward Growth, parents and professionals are encouraged to think about the soothing role of ritual/routine in life, and work to create a safe, functional ritual or routine in which to teach the skills that are needed to enjoy a social interaction. This is a principle that is very useful in individual interactions (see the example in Chapter 3 of the kindergarten student), but is absolutely vital in working with groups. When working with a group of students who have ASD, all the students will be challenged to remain regulated when a new game or concept is introduced. The ritual/routine will then become a kind of emotional security blanket that can envelop and support the students. Elements such as having the group meet on the same day, in the same place, in the same location, with the same leaders, with the same beginning and ending routines can be extremely valuable to the success of students. For some students this is an extremely high hurdle, and although they can manage to stay

---

2 Social Stories™ were developed by Carol Gray, and are used to teach children social cues and perspectives, and also to help children prepare for experiences that are relatively new to them. The reader can learn more about Social Stories by visiting www.thegraycenter.org.

regulated in a group, the introduction of any new activity results in a meltdown. These students benefit by having the adult introduce them to the new game or activity in individual sessions, so that when their group meets, the game is not new – the only new element is that there are now additional players. It is important for adults to think flexibly about how to provide enough ritual/routine so that the child feels safe in learning, while not creating ritual that is so rigid that the student melts down when any deviation takes place.

When students get older, they become less dependent on routine and can give up more control. But the need is still there. Groups should still try to meet at regular times, in regular places, and with familiar opening and closing rituals. It is important for adults not to lose sight of this.

An example is a recent experience at a local charter school. This school focuses on the educational needs of teens with ASD, and has hired me as a consultant. After discussing and experimenting with different formats, the school settled on a block schedule.[3] The block schedule cut down on the number of transitions in the day, significantly helping most of the students since almost all had difficulty ending something, packing material, moving to a new location, unpacking materials, and finally refocusing on a new subject.

In order to accommodate all the subjects that needed to be taught, the school made the decision that many other schools have made. They had alternating "A" days (in which a student has four classes) and "B" days (in which four different subjects are taught). When the school implemented this schedule, they ran into a significant problem. Many students had great difficulty managing their stress and anxiety owing to the fact that they could not count on particular days of the week being consistently "A" or "B" days. The fact that weekends and holidays caused the schedule to change was enough to stress many students significantly.

To its credit, the school chose not to blame the students for being rigid, but explored ways to support them. The solution was interesting. They added a "C" day.

The schedule ended up looking like this:

---

3   In a block schedule, there are four classes per day, each meeting for 80–90 minutes.

- Monday and Thursday would always be "A" days – the same four subjects taught.

- Tuesday and Friday would always be "B" days – the same four subjects taught.

- Wednesday was a "C" day – six of the above eight class taught for shorter time periods. They further determined that they would try to support their students by scheduling all field trips and community visits on Wednesdays – thereby further enhancing the reliability of the "A" day/"B" day routine.

Now this was not a perfect solution. Some students struggle on Wednesdays – but far fewer than used to struggle with the alternating day stresses. They provide those students with individualized supports, and the school functions well.

Parents can also use ritual or routine to help teach new skills while offering the comfort of the familiar. I have helped parents:

- Reduce homework wars by establishing a designated, time-limited homework time. The parent and child do schoolwork together during this time each day. If they finish early, they read together. If the homework takes more time, the parent writes the teacher a note that they "used up" all the homework time, so some homework is not going to be completed.

- Teach new games and activities by having a designated weekly "new fun time". The parent introduces a new activity or new component of an activity, and they play together for a designated time. This weekly event ends with the child choosing a favorite activity to do with the parent.

- Teach doing an activity in a new location or new time by having a designated "change up" time.

Because home life is less patterned and routine than school, parents often have to consider creating greater routine in order to have a structure in which they can introduce small changes. In what seems to be a paradox, ritual and routine need to be used in order to teach flexibility. In this way, we can all help individuals with ASD learn the important life skill of learning to stretch out of the need to keep things so tightly routine.

Chapter 6

Attention Challenges

It comes as no shock or surprise to anyone who deals with young people with ASD that almost all have challenges in attention skills. In the school district in which I worked, it was very common for students to first be identified/diagnosed with the medical diagnosis of attention-deficit hyperactivity disorder. Later, additional characteristics brought that child back to the medical doctor or to the special education team for consideration of an ASD. This may be the one hurdle that 100 percent of my clients share. The three most common attention challenges are:

- inattention
- hyper-attention
- difficulty shifting attention to orient to other activities or people.

My community-based groups (which the reader will learn about in Part III) are 90-minute programs that revolve around learning to be comfortable in the social world of having fun. We play a variety of games – the Wii, board games, card games, word games – and before we begin, we create a schedule that requires each participant to shift activities about every 20 minutes. In the creating of the schedule each week, my staff and I encounter the challenge of inattention.

Even though all the participants know the routine and know that we cannot start until we have a schedule, working through the scheduling process each week is challenging.

Since these are community-based groups, the participants arrive at slightly different times. Some will:

- buy a treat at the counter, and then become focused on eating and drinking
- bring a book to read while waiting for group to start
- begin to play with a hand-held video game they brought with them
- examine new game cards alone or with a friend
- pick up a magazine
- chat with another participant or with a staff member
- become interested alone or together in the wuzzles, commonyms, or logic puzzles I present each week on a whiteboard.[1]

We encourage all of the above, because it is a good skill to be able to occupy oneself while waiting to begin. However, the challenge then becomes establishing joint attention so that we might plan.

If you come to observe a group (and we are delighted to accommodate observers), you will see that we use various techniques to work on establishing joint attention. We encourage, we stop and wait, we remind, we suggest that participants move away from someone they are talking to or put down their cards or hand-held game – we do everything we can think of that is positive. We never demand or impose consequences for non-compliance. Even with our youngest participants in community groups, we begin to remind them gently that focusing jointly during a meeting is an employment skill. There will be meetings in every job and occupation, and the ability to attend to the topics of the meeting is a crucial job skill.

Now, we also encounter another common ASD characteristic during this part of our group. Some of our young people can actually attend to this organizing task better if they are looking at cards, reading, or playing their hand-held games. For a certain percentage of people with ASD, occupying the hands or the mind actually can

---

1   Wuzzles are combinations of drawings and words that represent common phrases. Commonyms are sequences of three words, all of which hold one word or phrase in common. Logic puzzles are word puzzles that require logic to be able to solve. All are available in books or on the internet.

increase attention skills.[2] I train my staff to be able to determine this through trial and error. We determine what is most helpful for each participant, and then coach that person to pay attention in the ways that works best for them.

This leads to some questions about fairness: "Why can Billy play his Gameboy but you are asking me not to?" I always answer by changing the question. I point out that I am not interested in establishing rules about the Gameboy, but I am interested in helping develop the skills at attending to the organizing task. So the question should be: "What helps me pay attention?" And then: "If it helps me, can I do it?"

The reality that some young people are helped to calm and to stay regulated by using manipulatives comes into consideration here. Many of our participants have been well served by occupational therapists and have their own objects that they use to touch, push, and/or manipulate in order to remain within their band of regulation. In considering the hurdle of establishing and maintaining attention, for some of these students, the very manipulatives that help them stay calm and regulated also keep the individual's attention on sensory input and not on the task or communication.

This is a dilemma. In these cases, my approach is to consider the need to stay calm and regulated to be a foundational skill, and one that should be protected. I try, however, to work with the young person to try out different objects and ways of getting sensory input in hopes of finding something that will assist with both calming *and* attending. Sometimes the answer is to wait – wait for the individual's brain to develop more and stronger neuropathways, and wait for the individual to develop more attention skills. Because I have often worked with young people for five, ten, and even 15 years, I have learned that noting an issue, but then being able to wait, can be a valuable and effective strategy.

Another aspect of attention that is challenging to the majority of the young people with whom I work is the skill of shifting attention from one area to another. When children with ASD are young, parents

---

2   These individuals need an advocate at school, because often the expectation is that students have everything off their desks and eyes on the teacher when the teacher is giving directions. The most extreme student I ever encountered was able to tell his teacher, "I can look at you or I can keep my head down, fidget and listen to you, but I can't do both. Which do you prefer?" The best teachers understand this to be true.

and school staff often struggle to get them started on a new task, and then, once on a task, to shift off that task – particularly if they are not finished with a task or activity. It is important to view this as a delay in the development of the skill of attention-shifting rather than a behavior issue.[3]

You will discover when you read about my group interventions that the structure of the groups promotes the development of attention-shifting as a skill. The youngest group members are constantly (and gently) asked to shift their attention from an activity, to the scoreboard, or from a role-play to the scoreboard. They are also asked to shift from a task to a decision about a reinforcer, and then back to task.

The older groups have many shifts. Board games are played in two-person teams, thus requiring participants to shift from the game to a discussion about strategy and then back again. Often the whole group is part of a team, requiring constant similar shifts. And, finally, the group is designed so that most games and activities are not completed, requiring the most difficult shift of all – ending the focus on the game before completion. Participants are enticed to make this shift by the strategic placement of the evaluation process, which rewards this skill with points that lead to a group reward.

With every group I do, I use whiteboards and graphics. These are aids to processing information, but are also invaluable in providing the opportunity to work on the skill of shifting attention. Asking the group to pause, consider a goal or statement on the whiteboard, and then resume provides two opportunities to work on attention-shifting skills.

---

3   This issue is often misidentified as a lack of cooperation in elementary skill, resulting in Individual Education Plans (IEPs) that include goals and objectives about cooperation. From my point of view, this is often a misidentification leading to the adults focusing on the wrong skill to teach and reinforce.

Chapter 7

Emotional Regulation Problems

Being able to modulate emotions – positive feelings such as excitement or enthusiasm, or negative feelings such as frustration or disappointment – in order to stay within the band of regulation is a skill that is slow to develop in most individuals with ASD. The fact is that many mental health providers do not have the opportunity to see enough individuals with ASD to allow them to understand this reality. This leads to many instances when a young person is diagnosed with either a mood disorder or a personality disorder. An important first step in providing effective emotional health support to persons with ASD is to understand that this delay exists. Once my clients begin to recognize aspects of their emotional life, it is time to gently begin to work on emotional control.

From my perspective, the skill of understanding and modulating our emotional state is a skill that every human being learns. Some of us are inclined to learn this easily and deeply – those might become poets or therapists. Others will struggle, but have the capacity to learn and keep learning. Most individuals with ASD are in the second group.

I train the clinical social workers, psychologists, and teaching staff who work with me to do a form of "upside down" therapy or counseling. I was trained to do traditional therapy – in short, working with individuals in order to help them come to recognize and then understand their emotions and motivations. The therapist helps the client stay clear and on track in this process, but the discovery is made by the client.

Because of the delays that individuals with ASD experience in understanding their emotions and motivations, the therapist or teacher is most often dealing on a much more basic level – as basic as simply correctly identifying emotions.

Think about the role that parents play with neurotypical infants and toddlers. We accept and understand that our children do not understand their emotional state, and that it is our job to recognize the differences between an "I'm hungry" cry, an "I'm tired" cry, an "I'm wet" cry, an "I'm lonely" cry, and so on. We do this and it leads to an important parent–child connection.

As a child begins to understand language, we begin to talk to our children as we deal with them, letting them know that we understand them and that right now they are tired, or lonely, or frustrated, or becoming ill with a cold. In doing that, we are also teaching them to recognize their emotional state. We are the teachers; they are the learners. As they progress in their learning, they begin to come to us and tell us what they are feeling. But they are making that assessment based on what they first learned from us.

Now, consider the child with ASD. This child has two significant delays – a delay in being able to recognize an emotional state, and, as we will discuss in Chapter 9, delays in being able to process the language necessary to process and communicate this information.

One clear evidence of this delay in most youngsters is an experience that almost every teacher of young elementary-age students with ASD has experienced. A student is doing relatively well – using the adaptations and supports that have been put in place and getting through most school days. Suddenly, that student has a day when everything falls apart, and the student melts down multiple times in situations that previously did not cause any stress.

The school staff members are baffled and concerned. Because they cannot identify any change or stressor at school, they assume that there must have been a stressful situation at home. Therefore, they note in the home–school notebook that the student has had a tough day and ask if the student had difficulty sleeping or if there has been any type of family disruption. They then wait for the next day to see what the parent will write in the notebook.

But then next day the student and the notebook do not arrive. Instead there is a voicemail that indicates that the child came home and reacted exactly the same. During the course of the late afternoon or evening, the parent placed a hand on the child's forehead or was able to take her temperature. The child's temperature was up. She was ill, and had been ill all day in school. The chills, body aches, and fever led to the child being irritable and distressed, which, understandably, had led to meltdowns. Everything now makes sense.

The delay in the child's ability to recognize a physical feeling led to that child being very uncomfortable. No child would choose this kind of discomfort – she simply lacked the skills to process the input from her body. The reality that this kind of delay exists in identifying a physical feeling indicates that most youngsters with ASD have similar or even greater difficulties identifying emotions.

Because this difficulty exists, the child also has difficulty processing emotions. Fear, anxiety, frustration and other stressors can cause a child or youth to come out of the band of regulation. This reality makes Social Stories for young children effective and powerful. Parents and teachers use Social Stories to prepare ASD students for experiences that occur outside of the comfort of the daily schedule – for example, going on a field trip. Social Stories tell about the facts. For example:

1. Tomorrow the schedule will be different.

2. At 10.15 we will end math class to get ready to go to the museum.

3. First we will go to the bathroom, and then put on our coats.

4. We will then line up and go to the bus.

5. We will ride the bus for 20 minutes and arrive at the museum.

The best Social Stories will also identify emotions. In doing this, the school staff are both preparing the student for the trip and also teaching about emotions – setting the stage for greater understanding and awareness. Note the addition of information about emotions:

1. Tomorrow the schedule will be different. *The change will feel both annoying and exciting.*

2. At 10.15 we will end math class to get ready to go to the museum. *It will be hard to stop math early, and you may be a little frustrated. But your paraprofessional will help you.*

3. First we will go to the bathroom and put on our coats.

4. We will then line up and go to the bus. *It may feel different or even a little scary because the bus will be loading in front of school instead of in the back, and it will not be the same bus you ride to school.*

5. We will ride the bus for 20 minutes and arrive at the museum. *The roads will be different and you may feel afraid. Your paraprofessional will sit next to you and you will have your favorite book to look at.*[1]

Helping young people recognize and understand emotions is an important skill that needs to be attended to long past early childhood, but the task becomes more difficult during the teen and early adult years. The individual has learned most of the more basic emotions, and now is dealing with the subtler emotional landscape of dealing with identity in a complex world.

I currently have a 17-year-old client whom I have known for three years. At times he has been in my *FunJoyment* groups, I consult at his school, and I now see him privately. David is currently taking an art class, and struggling – largely due to difficulty managing his emotions. David is both a perfectionist and extremely private. Being asked to express private thoughts/feelings in a piece of art, and then having an idea in his head but being unable to make it appear, cause him significant stress. When David feels stress at school, he has learned to blame the staff.[2] David was spending a lot of time blaming his art teacher. According to him, she was "stupid and inept". His assignments were "dumb, babyish, inappropriate, and too difficult". I have come to realize that David has reached his limit of understanding himself at school when he complains that, "my teachers just don't know how to teach". When he says that, I translate in my head that his emotions build, spill over, and are out of his ability to understand. According to

---

1   In extreme cases, a new route without any familiar landmarks can be very distressing. Having someone drive the route before the field trip day and take pictures of some of the sights and landmarks can help. The child and the paraprofessional can then look for the sights depicted in the photos, adding both a bit of familiarity to the trip and also giving the child something to focus on other than the distress of doing something new.

2   This is often the inadvertent effect of writing good "adaptations and modifications" when a child is young. The child learns that adults are supposed to read his emotional state, and make the changes necessary. Transitioning to doing this yourself can be difficult, so a teen can become "stuck" in a pattern of blaming adults when things become difficult.

David, his art teacher "doesn't know how to teach, never knew how to teach, and will never know how to teach". Clearly David felt the situation was out of his control.

My approach with clients is to ask questions designed to help me understand. If I can understand, I can help David understand. Knowing David for three years, and noting that his distress seemed magnified over his usual fear of revealing himself and not doing things perfectly, I was gently asking him some questions. At one point this occurred:

> John: Do you think the fact that she is young and pretty has anything to do with this?
>
> David: She is not young and she is not pretty.
>
> John: C'mon – she is barely in her 20s and she is quite pretty.
>
> David: She has got to be 60 – at least 50 – and she is not pretty. She is an old hag – a witch.

At that point I dropped the line of questioning because David was obviously upset and I risked locking him into a pattern if I pushed any further. But, based on this observation, I decided to pick up the thread sometime later about how David felt about girls and the world of dating. Sure enough, at a later session when I brought up the topic, David told me, "I don't know how to talk to girls. And even if I did, there are no good girls at my school." David and I have begun to explore the difficult landscape of male/female attraction and relationships. I most likely won't be able to help much in art, but I hope to help him in life.

Chapter 8

Organization Deficits

Organization of materials and oneself is a skill that is often portrayed as an indication of character. Especially in schools, teachers may appreciate and praise those students who have an innate inclination to develop organization skills. Students who lack the ability to master organization easily can end up feeling a bit second-rate. Teachers have a very difficult task. In addition to teaching academic skills, they are also teaching organization. Just as some students are more gifted in math, reading, or writing, for some students, organization comes easily.

It is interesting to think about the fact that many very intelligent adults eventually will take courses in organization or hire assistants to keep them organized. Many people do not develop a method of personal organization until college or well into a career. Have you ever noticed how individualized the desks, workspaces, and computers of professionals are? No two are alike, and when we sit at someone else's desk, the space seems foreign to us – nothing is quite where it "should" be. Yet people find information and materials at their own workstation with relative ease all the time.

So, organization is a skill, and it is a skill that is delayed in most individuals with ASD. Many children, in whose bedrooms we find all their toys and building materials uniquely organized, cannot find a homework assignment to save their lives. When students are young, we have paraprofessionals to help children pack and unpack backpacks every day. Despite the best efforts of school staff and parents, assignments (sometimes completed and ready for grading) and permission slips (often signed and ready to be turned in) end up lost forever.

In late elementary school and junior high, when students begin to move to different classrooms and different teachers, this delay causes frustration in students, teachers, and parents. In my workshops, I share two stories. Both are true. Both occurred right in front of my eyes. I was fortunate to have been invited into schools to assist with educational assessments by doing classroom observations of the individual students. Thus I had the luxury of focusing on a single student.

The first involves Jacki. Jacki attended a Montessori Junior High, and had done relatively well in elementary school. She was described in school records as being somewhat aloof, solitary, disorganized, and opinionated. In junior high, although obviously smart (she did very well on tests), she quickly fell so far behind in handing in assignments that she was in danger of failing. Fortunately, the school staff decided to do a special needs assessment, and, even more fortunately, they included in that assessment the elements needed to determine if Jacki was a student with ASD.

As part of my observations, I was in the back of a classroom watching Jacki in a language arts class. The class was correcting homework assignments from the previous night. When the correction was finished, the students were directed to pass the assignments forwards in the rows they were sitting. As I watched, the students at the very end of each row passed their paper to the person in front of them, who added their paper and passed to the next person. Jacki was in the middle of her row.

As I watched, Jacki took the papers from the student behind her, and passed the papers to the student in front of her. Her assignment remained on her notebook in front of her. Jacki then closed the notebook and put it away. At that point, I was the only person in the classroom who knew where the assignment was located.

The students were directed to read for the last ten minutes of class. During that time, the teacher had a few student assistants go through the assignments and record that they had been turned in. Then, with five minutes before lunch, the teacher read a list of five names and announced that those students had the assignment missing and would not be allowed to go to lunch until it was turned in. Jacki's name was called.

Jacki had assertive skills, and she used them. She charged right up to the teacher and told him that she had indeed turned in her work. The teacher did the logical thing – he handed Jacki the stack of assignments and told her to find hers. I watched, with a combination of interest and apprehension, as Jacki plowed through the stack – twice. She was baffled that hers was missing and told the teacher so.

At that point Jacki caught a break. The teacher gently suggested that she go back to her desk and look in her notebook. Jacki initially resisted because she was positive she had turned the work in, but eventually she went back to her desk, opened her notebook, and saw the missing assignment. At that point, the look on her face indicated that she had just witnessed magic – her paper had flown out of the collected stack and found its way back into her notebook! Astonished, Jacki handed the assignment in and joined her classmates who were lining up for lunch.

Rick attended a local public junior high and had failed classes during the school year due to lack of completion of assignments. I was invited to observe and then interact with him in summer school. Eventually, I discovered that Rick had significant language processing and writing difficulties, but, before that happened, I observed him in his summer math class.

I was again stationed at the rear of the classroom. The class had been working on a worksheet and most were using calculators. Rick was using a classroom calculator – easily distinguished by its size and bright blue color. When he finished the assignment, Rick took the calculator and placed it on the rack under his desk. A few minutes later the teacher announced that the work period was over, and asked everyone to hand in their assignment sheets. Rick handed in his sheet. The teacher then held up the classroom rack for calculators and announced that seven were still out. He asked that they be returned. Rick sat quietly in his desk.

A few minutes later the teacher announced there were still three calculators out. Rick was still sitting quietly. A minute later, the teacher said, "I'm still missing a calculator." Rick did not move.

At this point, the teacher spotted the calculator under Rick's chair. He did a very wise and gracious thing. He walked down the aisle and picked it up. Rick did not notice and the teacher remained silent. I was grateful – I was convinced that once Rick placed the calculator under his seat, he lost track of it. When the teacher asked for calculators to be handed in, Rick probably scanned his desk. Not spotting a calculator, he most likely assumed he had handed it in. Out of sight, out of mind. Clearly this was an organizational issue.

These types of delays in the ability to be able to learn to organize affect the students I work with in high school and when they begin in community college. Once their brains have developed to the point of being able to learn an organizational skill, many teachers are no longer teaching organization because most of their students have developed this skill. Fortunately, there are special education teachers who step in to teach this important skill and thus free the classroom teacher to focus on content.

When the students I work with learn an organizational skill, they often have difficulty generalizing it to a different project or class. I have had students learn the small steps needed to research, write and outline, and then present a topic using PowerPoint. However, when many of these students are asked to do the same initial and intermediate steps in order to write a paper, many have great difficulty understanding that the initial and intermediate steps are the same, because the end product is so different. They need help learning a process; they then need help learning to generalize on something they have learned.

Many students have difficulty with the transition from high school to college, even though teachers and parents have been trying to explain to them or prepare them for months. A frequent occurrence in my practice is for one of my clients to do very poorly in the first semester or two of college, and then begin to do well.[1] High school and college students with ASD seem to learn best by doing – and, sometimes, doing also includes failing.

---

1   In addition to having difficulty learning how to organize materials and time in order to do satisfactory work in college, most of my clients have not been able to take what is considered a full load. They can do fine as part-time students, but cannot stay on top of the work load when taking the course work expected as a full-time student. At this time, I counsel all my clients and their parents to: 1. try to enter a transition program that will help the students learn college and life skills, and 2. begin by taking about half the number of courses suggested for full-time students. From my point of view, it is better to take a few more years to get an associate or bachelor's degree than to fail to finish and be scared off from ever attending college again.

Chapter 9

Language Processing Issues

Difficulties processing language have long been understood to be a hallmark characteristic of an autism spectrum disability. In Minnesota, perhaps the most important early intervention specialist sent into homes of children assessed with ASD by physicians and/or school districts is the speech/language pathologist. Early in my career, the professionals most helpful to me in learning to adapt my skills to working with students with ASD were my colleagues in the speech/language realm. One of the first things they told me was: "Stop talking so much. You are explaining too much. Show, don't explain." To this day, when I watch myself on videotape, the most common criticism I make of myself is that I am talking too much.

When I began formulating the groups that are described in Part III of this book, I worked closely with speech/language pathologists. For the first ten years of my work developing groups, each group was co-led by a speech/language professional and me. The pairing of mental health and speech/language professionals is still the recommendation I make to school districts beginning to use *FunJoyment* groups. However, in today's funding environment of tighter budgets, few are able to recreate this combination. I still believe that the combination of the two perspectives creates the best environment for the two professionals to learn from each other, and that the long-term benefits of creating the pairing will pay off in high-quality services.

Regardless, young people with ASD have language processing issues. For most, this is a significant hurdle. When I work with clients, I look for three different possible issues:

- expressive language

- receptive language

- ritualized Language.

Expressive language difficulties

Delays in expressive language take many forms and are easiest to observe in young children. In its most basic form, this delay is noted in toddlers by a delay in the development of speech. In doing developmental interviews, it is very common to have parents speak about a delay in speech, as well as an uneven or unusual pattern of speech development. By the time I would meet students in kindergarten, this was often evident in delays in using pronouns, tenses of verbs, and/or adjectives and adverbs. In addition, students also had difficulty with synonyms, antonyms, and in generalizing language – for example, looking at a picture book and learning that a structure is a barn, but then not being able to generalize that concept to another book when a barn is depicted in a slightly different manner. All the early elementary students with whom I worked on social interaction and social enjoyment had regular sessions with the speech/language pathologist, and all were working hard on being able to use language to express their thoughts.

As mentioned in Chapter 7, most youngsters have difficulty learning how to recognize feelings and then to express them. My speech/language colleagues were hard at work on this as well.

Expressive language difficulties continue into the late elementary and teen years, but are generally subtler. These students have learned to use pronouns, verb tenses, and modifiers, and have made progress in generalizing. The most common characteristic I encounter is difficulty ordering the sequences in an event and expressing them in the logical sequence. When students are doing an oral book report, they will often have all the facts correct, but start the story in the middle, move to the end, and then tell the beginning. This difficulty can lead to lowered grades, but can have even more serious consequences when dealing with police and authority figures.

I worked with Kent during his entire high school career. Kent enjoyed school, and he especially loved everything German. He collected German and Nazi memorabilia. Although he struggled to pass, he enrolled in German language classes.

One day Kent arrived at my group very upset – so upset that I had my staff begin group and I sat with Kent and his mom and listened to his story. Kent had been accused of stealing the German III final exam because he had not turned in his final,[1] and was suspended from school. When I asked Kent to tell me the story, he, predictably, began in the middle. He talked about being sent to the office and being accused of stealing, next talked about taking the final, switched back to how hard the final test was, talked about remembering exactly how he had turned in the test, and then moved to the "unfairness" of the suspension. Because I had worked with clients in difficult situations like this before, I listened carefully and took notes so I could sequence the events for myself.

After listening for about 15 minutes, I began to ask Kent questions designed to help me fill in the blanks of his story and to clarify that I was understanding accurately. This was also a bit difficult, because Kent had difficulty sequencing the answers to my questions. We had spent about ten minutes on this when Kent, in answering a question about handing in his test, made this comment: "I think I put it on the right desk."

That statement triggered a thought in my mind. I remembered that Kent's high school, like many high schools in Minnesota, often have rooms that multiple teachers use during the course of a day, and that in those rooms there is often more than one teacher desk. I asked Kent if that was the case in his German classroom. He told me that it was, and at the beginning of the test the teacher had written on the board that students should put their completed test on her desk, and then they were free to leave. He further reflected that he was a bit confused when it came time to turn in his test, because he was one of the last students to finish, and two other students had entered the room to talk to the teacher. When Kent finished his test, the teacher was sitting on the teacher desk nearest the door, chatting with the students. During class, he reflected, she usually sat at the other desk, but because she was at the desk by the door, Kent assumed she wanted the test turned in right by her. He placed it on the desk behind his teacher and left the room.

---

1   The school authorities believed that Kent had failed to turn in his final exam in order to take it and either show it or sell it to students who would be taking the same final later that day or on the following day.

Kent then looked at me and asked, "Do you think I put it on the wrong desk?" I told him I did and asked his mom to call the school first thing in the morning and ask the teacher to look on the desk by the door. She did, and there she found Kent's exam.

I had done nothing remarkable except patiently listen to and work to understand Kent's story. I helped him sequence it and helped him realize that he made a wrong assumption.

Receptive language difficulties

Decoding the spoken language of others can be a lifetime difficulty for individuals dealing with ASD. Once again, this is easiest to see in very young children, and our videotaped office assessments often will reveal the difficulty young children have processing even simple directions. Many times they struggle with understanding directions to put something under, on, or behind pieces of furniture in our office. We can then demonstrate how helpful it is to write or draw the direction. With this assistance, most children do much better. It is my observation that many of what may appear to be behavior problems can be better understood as receptive language issues. Most teachers give directions verbally, and difficulty processing the verbal instructions and directions can lead to misunderstandings. Compliance can be significantly improved when the teacher uses a graphic, writes the direction on the board, or gives the student individualized written or visual directions.

Again, as students get older and master rudimentary skills, receptive language difficulties can be masked. Students quickly learn that if a teacher asks, "Do you understand?" the best answer is always "Yes!" – even if you do not understand – because there are rarely follow-up questions. Their desire to avoid being singled out in class can work against the mastery of the lesson.

When directions and information are often given verbally, in a long sequence, and at a rapid rate, students with ASD can fall behind the flow of information. Adults are often fooled into thinking that because a young person can understand one complex sentence in isolation, she can process a series of directions or elements of a presentation. Sometimes the problem is the delay in the development of the skills needed to organize the information in the student's head. Sometimes the difficulty is processing verbal information at the speed at which it is typically delivered in a junior high or high school classroom.

I try never to assume that the youth I work with can process and organize what I am saying at the speed I am saying it. I travel with three whiteboards in my car, and I bring them into every situation in which I interact with students. I use them in groups and while engaged in both individual and family therapy. Writing on the whiteboards is the best way I know to give my clients both verbal and visual information.

Because most junior and senior high students with ASD process best when clear visual information is presented along with verbal information, I counsel students and parents to seek out those teachers who provide PowerPoint presentations as part of their regular classroom procedure, and encourage them to ask teachers to provide a handout of each presentation for the student to have right on his desk. My clients are often unready to succeed in a class that includes significant amounts of discussion/debate. Class discussion is a legitimate and valued form of teaching, but it is much better suited to neurotypical students than to students with ASD.

Ritualized language

Many students with ASD memorize and ritualize language. This is most easily recognized in the echolalia[2] of young children. Many times the only way we can get young children to be successful in my *FunJoyment* groups is actually to give them the phrase, statement, or question they need to participate in the role-play, and simply have them repeat it. We are more than willing to do so since the goal of the group is to have them learn the skills needed to enjoy a social interaction. My colleagues in the speech/language business will continue their efforts to help these students progress beyond echolalia in their individual speech time.

As students progress, we see many continuing patterns of interactions – often using the same compliments or verbal ways of interacting with peers week after week. We take a gentle approach to this – simply making sure that every few weeks a student is paired with an adult leader in a partner activity. During those times, the adult partner models a new way of asking a question or making a statement. Our goal is to give the student a large enough repertoire of memorized statements that she can better approximate the more spontaneous speech of her peers.

---

2   This is a condition in which a person is compelled to repeat the words spoken by someone else.

Chapter 10

Associative Thinking

Associative thinking can best be illustrated using a game my family used to play on long car rides. We called it "Word Association". I've heard others call it "Free Association". Basically, two or more people try to create associations to single words. For example:

John: Black.

Nick: White.

John: Bread.

Nick: Money.

John: Loan.

Nick: Shark.

John: Ocean.

Nick: Beach.

John: Hawaii.

Nick: Island…

…and on and on until we begin to laugh or repeat ourselves.

Most individuals with ASD excel at associative thinking – very often associating to their favorite topics areas and sometimes talking at length about that association, ignoring verbal and non-verbal signals that neurotypical peers are no way near as interested in or amused by that particular topic.

In classrooms, associative thinking can lead to situations that frustrate teachers while leading classmates to laughter. A discussion about the tactics and strategy of World War II might lead a teacher to lecture about the German warship *Bismarck*, and the danger it posed to Allied shipping once it had slipped into the North Atlantic. The presentation would continue leading to the fact that the British Navy succeeded in sinking the *Bismarck*. At that point, the eager hand of a student with ASD might shoot into the air, and the teacher, pleased that the student was listening and following the presentation, would call on the student. The student could very likely proudly make a statement such as "The Titanic sunk, too!"

The other students would likely chuckle, and the teacher might get upset because of the "off topic" comment. The proud student might be confused or might even feel reinforced and pleased by the laughter and the attention of the teacher.

Schools teach and reinforce logical, sequential thinking. In math, lessons build on the preceding lessons. In language arts and social science classes, students are taught to write papers by presenting evidence and then progressing to a logical, step-by-step explanation about how the evidence leads to a logical conclusion. Leaping from one idea to another with no connection in between can seem impulsive. It may be, but then again it might not be.

I have heard a story – it may be real or may be apocryphal – about a young Albert Einstein walking toward a church in his village in Germany as the bell in the steeple begins to ring. He looked at the steeple, and his gaze continued to a hill a few miles outside of the town. And he had the associative thought that if he were standing on that hill, he would not be hearing the bell at that same moment. It occurred to him that some things are relative – a thought he continued to think about, and apply logic to understanding, for many years before he proposed the Theory of Relativity – which was initially ridiculed by his colleagues.

Whether or not that story is true, it is clear that mankind has benefited by associative thoughts that lead to leaps that would not be reached by applying slow, deliberate, logical thinking. Here are a few examples.

In 1932, a young woman with little formal medical training, but a passion for helping that led her to work as nurse for Australian troops in World War I, created a backyard clinic in a small town in Australia for polio patients. There she shunned the casts, braces, and bed rest that were the accepted medical intervention of the day and made the leap to hot baths, heat treatment, passive movement, and muscle massage. She got dramatic, positive results. However, members of the medical establishment viciously attacked her methods. She continued in spite of the criticism, eventually traveling to my home state of Minnesota, getting support from the Mayo Clinic, and eventually establishing what became the world-renowned Sister Kenny Institute in Minneapolis.

In the late 1970s and early 1980s, two Australian medical doctors noticed something curious about their patients suffering with stomach ulcers, and, in studying the pathology, made the associative leap to the theory that ulcers might be caused by a virus. Once again the medical community rallied to discredit their methods and research. In a leap in research protocol, one of these doctors deliberately infected, and then cured, himself. This move was also roundly ridiculed. In 2005 the Nobel Prize in Medicine went to Dr. Robin Warren and Dr. Barry Marshall for their pioneering work in correctly identifying that a virus caused stomach ulcers and helping millions of people recover from that virus.

In the early 1960s, a gawky teen in Medford, Oregon, wanted to excel in a sport. After trying different sports, he eventually focused on the high jump, but had great difficulty mastering the straddle technique, which was then recognized worldwide as the premier jumping technique. One day, it occurred to him that he could do better running to the bar, then turning his back and going over backwards. Although he did indeed jump much better, his high school coach, and eventually his college coach, persisted in trying to get him to abandon his technique and return to the straddle. Fortunately, he refused. In 1968, Dick Fosbury, with no coach because no one knew the technique he had invented better than him, won gold at the Olympics. Today all jumpers use the "Fosbury flop".

Now, certainly not every associative thought leads to world-shaking results. My wife's father was born shortly after the turn of the century. Before Clarence died, he liked to tell the story about "The cart that always ran downhill".

During that age of great mechanical innovation, he and his brother noticed that carts and wagons would always roll freely downhill. One day, they had the "genius" thought that if they created a wagon with large wheels in the back and short wheels in the front, the bed of the cart would slant back to front – thus creating a perpetual "downhill" on which the cart would roll. With great enthusiasm and industry, they managed to procure two large wheels, two small wheels, rope, and lumber. They took their supplies out to a clear field that had a large tree. After building the bed of their cart, they cleverly tied the bed to the tree to keep everything safe. They then fashioned two axles which they attached to the cart – large wheels in the rear, and small wheels in front.

Because Sharon's dad was younger, he did not get the first ride. With the older brother on the cart, Clarence's job was to slice the rope with an ax. He did – and nothing happened. It had been a great associative thought, but the theory obviously did not work.

More often, as in the examples above, the theory is correct, but logical thinking must be applied before the theory can be proved. Before the Wright brothers, many inventors (all the way back to Leonardo da Vinci) had dreamed and schemed to achieve flight. Movies exist depicting the efforts that immediately preceded the Wright brothers – fanciful contraptions and daredevil pilots. All ended in crashes and tragedies.

The Wright brothers were more than dreamers and inventors. They were engineers. They envisioned a wing, and used calculus to perfect it. They then did something even more amazing. They envisioned a propeller as a wing that spun – but spun at different speeds as the propeller extended out from the shaft. Due to that fact, the "wing" of the propeller had to change its shape as it moved towards the edge in order to create maximum "lift". Again, they logically used calculus to bring an associative thought to reality. They dreamed, but then they worked hard.

My colleagues and I define associative thinking to our clients. We point out the benefits (intellectual enjoyment, some remarkable breakthroughs like the ones described above), but after defining that we let them know that they also have to learn the power of logical thinking – because it is the linear and logical thinking that allows those who make the great leaps to be able to prove their theories. In all the examples above, once the individuals had made the associative leap, they needed to apply logic and discipline to "proving" their theories. I see associative thinking and linear thought as complementary processes.

I also counsel teachers to understand and appreciate associative thinking, and to do two things in the classroom:

1. Provide coaching, mentoring and support as my associative thinkers work their way through linear classes. They will have difficulty with this, and their skills will usually lag behind neurotypical peers.

2. Help the rest of the students understand, and even value, the associative gifts of these young people.

Chapter 11

Sensory Sensitivities[1]

Persons with ASD typically process sensory information differently. This presents challenges to their ability to learn and work in the environments that we have created and consider typical. As with many other hurdles, this one is most evident and presents the most challenge when individuals are young. But the challenges remain throughout their lives.

When I do developmental interviews for clients in my office and interact with participants in my groups, I am always gathering information about the way they interact with the sensory world. I think about the five senses – vision, hearing, taste, smell, and touch – but also proprioception and the awareness they have about the way their whole body feels internally.

Vision

Many of my clients prefer lower levels of light, and some avoid being outside on clear days due to the brightness. Different kinds of lighting can be problematic with persons with ASD – both the intensity of the light and the way it is generated. I have had clients insist they can see, and are very distracted by, the "flickering" of fluorescent lighting. Many students prefer to wear hats with bills or visors in all situations.

When I do developmental interviews and am discussing vision issues, I always ask about early play patterns that involved lining up

---

1   As mentioned in Chapter 4, just about everyone will recognize that they have some difficulty with one or more of the hurdles. This hurdle is one that many neurotypical individuals experience. Again the difference is a matter of degree. This is a significant issue for many of my clients.

cars, building blocks, markers or other objects. I also ask about the phenomenon of staring at the spinning wheels of toy cars or the spinning blades of fans at this time.

Vision sensitivities present significant challenges for preschool and early elementary teachers. Often the visual environment that enriches the experience for neurotypical students overloads youngsters with ASD.

Hearing

Auditory issues and preferences are often a part of the profile for individuals with ASD. In addition to seeming to have a narrow band of comfort for auditory input (very little gap between what is too soft to be heard and what is so loud that it "hurts" the ears), many sounds in the ambient environment are harder to process. Many young children have great difficulty with emergency vehicle sirens and can become truly distressed with alarms and warning alerts. Very often great care must be taken during fire and emergency weather drills when students are young, and I have observed many secondary students who hold their hands over their ears (or wear headphones or sound-dampening devices) during drills.

Outside of schools, the sound systems at malls, restaurants and especially movie theaters can be set at a level that is too loud for youngsters with ASD.[2] Families often need to plan carefully for outings, and schools need to think about the sound level when they take students on school field trips.

Another auditory issue that is often present for young people with ASD is their awareness (and annoyance) with noises in the environment while they are trying to focus on homework. The noise of a TV in the basement or a sibling talking on the phone can become a stressor to the point of a meltdown. This presents obvious challenges to a family. Often the short-term remedy is setting up a quiet, private place for the child to do homework, and providing some soundproofing to that space, or sound-dampening ear protection for the child to wear.

---

2   The Autism Society of Minnesota regularly schedules movies in theaters with the sound level dampened considerably so that families of children that are particularly sensitive can enjoy a movie together.

Fortunately, most children grow in their ability to tolerate ambient sounds as they age.

Taste

Almost every young person I have ever worked with has some type of issue around eating – many relating to taste, but others relating to texture and temperature. Young children with ASD can have a very limited number of foods that they will eat, and that can be compounded by their desire to have foods at the "correct" temperature and texture. There seems to be no definite pattern – I have known children who loved bananas because they are "soft", and children who have hated bananas because they are "squishy". Some of my clients regularly eat macaroni and cheese – but some will only eat the kind made from the packet, and some will only eat the microwave variety.

These preferences can obviously create huge problems when families want to eat out. Many children with ASD will refuse to eat restaurant food, or will only eat at certain restaurants. The most creative and assertive of the parents that I work with have worked things out with a few restaurants so that the family can order off the menu and then the one child with ASD brings in a bag lunch.

The taste issue presents unique challenges in some of my groups. Sometimes a youth will celebrate a birthday at one of my groups. (For some of my teen participants, the *FunJoyment* group peers are the logical group for the party, so parents ask to schedule it as part of the group.) Often, the desired food is pizza, most often cheese, but then we have the challenge that, even with cheese pizza, the group members have strong preferences for certain brands. No matter what ends up being ordered, we usually have some group members choose not to eat.

At their extreme, significant eating preferences can be a limiting and complicating factor in a child's development and in a family's functioning. In extreme cases, I have found that referring to an occupational therapist with expertise in eating issues is often the most successful intervention. A child with an extremely narrow band of food interests can usually be "stretched", but it is an issue that will most likely be a lifelong challenge.

Smell

The issues with smells in an environment seem to be similar to what most neurotypical individuals experience, just more extreme. Like all of us, individuals have certain smells that they prefer, and certain smells that they dislike. Their response (again, more likely with younger individuals) can be much more extreme – melting down when encountering a non-preferred smell; becoming hyper alert and attentive to a preferred smell – and they can respond to odors at a level that can seem imperceptible to their neurotypical parents and siblings.

This, like taste, can result in a family having to do additional planning in order to make visits to stores, restaurants, and the homes of friends and relatives a successful experience. It also requires a school to be thoughtful about a cooking demonstration, science experiment, or field trip to a location with olfactory input.

Touch

Although many individuals prefer the touch of some fabrics over others (I have always avoided wool, regardless of how cold I am), this sense provides multiple, and heightened, issues for most of my clients. In short, this is what I have encountered:

- difficulty tolerating tags and seams in articles of clothing

- difficulty with articles of clothing that are tight or stiff

- a preference for short sleeves over long, and short pants over long

- a preference to wear the same articles of clothing every day

- a reluctance to wear anything new or throw out anything that has become worn out or no longer fits

- a reluctance to zip or button coats and jackets

- a reluctance to wear hats, gloves, or mittens no matter how cold the weather

- a preference to sleep on top of comforters and blankets rather than under them.

In addition to these issues around clothing, many of my clients:

- prefer not to be touched or hugged – or at least like to be warned that a touch or hug is about to occur

- can seek ways of getting pressure on their bodies that are under control – for example, weighted vests, weighted blankets, lying under gym mats while the teacher applies pressure

- need to wash their hands immediately if they get dirty, and sometimes want to change clothes if they become soiled

- prefer not to touch materials in art class (clay, paint, paste, glue) that many other students enjoy

- either really like or really dislike showers

- enjoy the full body pressure of being in a swimming pool (but only if the pool is the "right" temperature).

Again, all these issues lead to the reality that families and professionals need to understand these requirements and plan when young people are entering new or different environments.

Proprioception

Proprioception is the sense we have of where parts of our body are in the relative space around us – without visually checking. A good way of thinking about it is to think about the field sobriety checks that police use to determine if an individual might have been drinking and is impaired. They ask an individual to do things such as:

- walk a straight line, heel-to-toe, without looking down

- close eyes, stretch out arms, and then touch the nose with the tip of an index finger.

Alcohol and chemical use can make doing the above hard. Many individuals with ASD have significant difficulty with this awareness without using any alcohol or chemicals.

A delay in proprioception is a characteristic of ASD, leading to the common reality that many youngsters have significant delays in being able to do the basic physical tasks (throwing, kicking, catching) that are required in athletic activities. Most youngsters with ASD have difficulty learning these skills (as well as the complicated game and social rules of many team sports) and thus in participating on community sports teams.[3]

The best consistent example of difficulty with proprioception in my experience was the difficulty my elementary students had learning to ride bicycles. Many were successful with tricycles and enjoyed vehicles and speed, but were very unsuccessful, and eventually discouraged, when they tried to learn to ride a bike. The adaptive physical education teacher and I would often face a special education goal of learning to ride a bicycle. We found this challenging, because we had no resources different from those available to parents.

One year my son had just outgrown his small first bicycle, and we brought it into the gym to give us something to practice on. One day, when I was thinking about my developing philosophy that we needed to break things into smaller and smaller steps, I had an idea. It occurred to me that, because of the difficulty with proprioception, we might want to break the task into first learning to balance, and then learn to propel and brake at a later time. In watching the students, I realized that the pedals sticking out of the bike got in the way of kids putting their feet down in order to prevent falling.

We decided to take the pedals off, and let the students use the bike as a scooter. In doing so, we broke the task down into learning to steer and balance first, and we also reduced the possibility of falling. Once the students mastered "scooting", we introduced the concept of "scooting" to get to a good speed, and then lifting both feet to glide. Once they had mastered the glide, we put the pedals back on and introduced propulsion and braking.

---

3   Although I occasionally have a client who excels in the physical skills of a team sport, and also learns the complex rules, I often steer clients to individual and somewhat repetitive sports. Many of my clients have enjoyed competitive swimming, track and field, tennis, fencing, and bocce ball. Many others play on teams that adapt to individual differences.

The process was not easy. It was time consuming, but it did result in most students being interested and successful enough to remain motivated to keep trying, and most eventually learned to ride.[4]

Whole body feel

This is a term I developed myself in order to explain a phenomenon that my school colleagues and I often saw – especially with younger students. As mentioned in Chapter 7, there seems to be a delay in ability to recognize and understand that a person might be dealing with an illness. Many students appeared to have difficulty recognizing that they might be feeling ill. We would be alerted to a possible health difficulty by a student beginning to melt down. We often would then ask our nurse at school or the parent at home to take the child's temperature, look at the child's eyes and throat, and/or look for any other outwards signs of illness.

Over time, young people gain awareness of their own body's signals around illness. I suspect this is also true for other "whole body" issues – for example, the ache caused by physical exertion, the "dullness" caused by interrupted or too little sleep, or the restlessness caused by too much sugar intake on holidays or at birthday parties. Again, it is not that young people with ASD cannot do this identification, but that many have a delay in the development of this skill.

---

4   At this point most families discovered that attention difficulties could have major safety implications in bike-riding. Many youngsters concentrated so hard on balance and technique that they failed to attend to the environment. Others mastered balance, but would notice a dog or a building and become interested, and in doing so forget to check the immediate environment. For many parents, biking became a family activity that required the parent to be with the youngster and constantly reminding about things to pay attention to.

This turned out to be a good lesson for both the youngsters and the parents when it came time to consider learning to drive a car. Many of my clients do not drive or drive with extreme care.

Chapter 12

"Unlearning" Rituals

As all of you who parent or work with young people with ASD are well aware, these are individuals who thrive on ritual and routine. This is a positive when we have figured out how to help someone manage the hurdles he faces and stay solidly within his band of regulation. However, as we all know, when things get difficult, a less than functional behavior pattern can become a comfortable routine or ritual.

Within my system, when an individual struggles, the first thing I recommend to professionals is to do what I call *ignore/observe*. Rather than follow the impulse that most of us have to intervene with a verbal correction or the threat of a negative consequence, the best first step is usually to do as little as possible while observing. This is one of the reasons that it is beneficial to have two trained professionals involved in a group. If a participant has difficulty – for example, leaving her chair, shouting, poking at the child next to her – one person can quietly move to sit next to the student and either interrupt the negative interaction, or leave the group to keep eyes on the participant who has left the circle.[1] It is also helpful to have a paraprofessional or special education teacher in a classroom setting so that the lesson can continue while gentle intervention and observation are also taking place.

The value of the ignore/observe technique is twofold. One, the off-task or disruptive behavior might be a just a singular event, and by not providing any negative attention to it, the professionals avoid

---

1   When this happens, it is important for the other leader to use immediately the reinforcements that are built into the group process (see Part III for descriptions of the group process) in order to clearly demonstrate to the on-task members that their behavior and participation is noted and valued.

inadvertently reinforcing the behavior and making it more likely that the behavior will reoccur. Youngsters with ASD tend to notice if they have done something that has caused excitement and gained the attention of those around them, but have a very poor sense of when they are getting positive attention and when that attention is negative. Therefore, any attention will most likely tend to reinforce a behavior.

The second reason to ignore/observe is to gain the time to observe, and after observation, to begin to understand which hurdle(s) have been encountered. Once that determination has been made, a constructive plan can be created.

However, with the passage of time, the risk is that by the time the adults feel they have an understanding of the roots of the difficulty and are ready to intervene, there is an additional hurdle. The off-task behavior may have become a comfortable ritual. The act of simply walking into the classroom or group room might trigger the ritual behavior. In such a case, the adults should be ready to reward.

I know that cultural critics have identified systemic problems with an emphasis on rewarding children, and have argued that many children are actually hindered in their long-term development by an emphasis on rewards. But I am talking about using a reward when we are trying to help a person give up a comfortable ritual or routine. We do this for ourselves – setting a reward is often the way that we encourage ourselves to stick to plans to save money, lose weight, or stop smoking.

An important aspect of using rewards in this fashion is involving the youth in understanding the process, in setting the goal, and in evaluating progress. The process I use is this:

1. I sit down with the individual and identify the problem behavior. I let him know that we are going to work together to create a solution.[2]

2. I never ask the youngster to simply stop something. I think simply stopping is the most difficult of all behavior change.

---

2   The amount of participation I expect from the youngster is proportional to the age and skill level of that youth. For a very young or very delayed individual, the participation I expect is simply for them to listen while I explain (using whiteboard drawings) the problem and the solution behavior that I have devised. For high school students, the process is much more a mutual discussion, but I still use a whiteboard to record our ideas and make sure that we leave with the same understanding.

Instead I/we develop an alternative replacement behavior (e.g. holding a fidget instead of poking a peer, or getting up, crossing the room, and looking at a picture book instead of yelling and knocking over the chair).

3. We then practice the replacement behavior we have agreed upon. We practice at a time when there is little stress. For example, I might invite the youngster into my room when there is no group meeting and we practice in the group setting without the distraction and excitement of the other participants. I always reward the student for practicing.[3]

4. Once the replacement behavior has been practiced in isolation, I move the practice to the group or classroom setting where the problem behavior has occurred. But we do not wait for a student to become stressed; the student and I identify a time at which the student will practice the replacement behavior. The student watches the clock, and, at the agreed upon time, the teacher or I signal the student. The student does the replacement behavior, and points toward the reward are earned.

5. There is one more stage in practicing before we attempt to do the replacement behavior under stress. At this stage the student knows that the adult is going to signal that the replacement behavior should be practiced, but does not know exactly when the signal will come. This way, we add the stress of limited surprise. Again, points are earned toward a reward.

6. Use the replacement behavior under the actual stressful circumstance. (I generally offer double or even triple the points for success at this stage.)

The most successful experience I ever had using this technique involved a 19-year-old boy in a transition program. Clint was a very

---

3   Although I might begin a relationship with a youngster by rewarding with a piece of candy, stickers, or trinkets, I try to move to "relationship" rewards as quickly as I can. The relationship reward I try to move to is time to play a favorite game or activity, first with me and eventually with selected peers. When I do this, I move to a point system in which each practice is worth a certain number of points, and when a target number is attained, the reward is earned. I never take points away – if the individual refuses to practice or does a poor job in practice, the consequence is no points earned rather than points being taken away.

bright, slightly built, and usually energetic young man who had been excluded from every school he had attended since junior high for threatening and aggressive behavior toward students and staff. In short, when Clint lost it, he really lost it. His language was vile and his fists flew. I was called in to consult after he had been unsuccessful in three high schools, and was placed in a special education transition program that provided him access to a local community technical college.

Clint was doing okay in his college math and electricity classes, but was losing it at the transition program. His parents and I were called into a meeting at which some members of staff at the program were advocating that he be excluded because he used such vulgar language toward the staff. It did not help that Clint became upset at the meeting and let loose with an obscenity-laced tirade about how he was going to rip the director of the program limb from limb.

The next day Clint and I discussed the situation, and I noted two things. One, Clint was very reasonable and took responsibility for his behavior, and, two, when I reflected this to him, he casually stated, "Yeah, I'm always able to do that the day after I lose it, but I'm never able to do it the day I get upset."

Using the system I outlined above, Clint and I devised a system that included the following elements:

- We would ask the program to identify a space that would always be available to Clint if he became upset.

- We would stock that space with things that Clint would use to both relax and take his mind off the incident that upset him – we decided on a 300-piece jigsaw puzzle, a novel, and a CD player.

- Clint would commit to always going to the space if he became upset, and further commit to staying there until the end of the school day – which could be hours if an incident happened in the morning.

- We would ask the staff to leave Clint alone in his space.

- Clint would promise to sit down with staff and reasonably process the incident the next day.

I was shocked at how calmly and reasonably Clint participated in creating the plan, and how confident he was that he could do it. He readily agreed to some practice sessions that would, we hoped, convince the staff that Clint would manage himself. I admit that it was a much tougher task getting the staff of the transition program to agree to give the plan a chance. They predicted failure, but I convinced them that they had nothing to lose, and they dutifully set up a "Clint table" in a sitting area just off the main office.

Clint practiced and did well. And then an incident happened. Late one morning, a student teased Clint about being skinny and wearing glasses, and Clint responded by threatening to kill the student. When an adult intervened, Clint told that adult to "f___ off". The adult then told Clint it looked like a time to go to his table. Clint went to the table and sat there for three hours. The next morning he came in, calmly admitted he was wrong to threaten the student and swear at the teacher, and asked what his consequences would be. The administrator was so shocked that she suggested that, in this case, apologies to the student and staff person would be the only requirement. Clint did both. He remained in the program and graduated with a high school diploma that spring.

His success continues to inspire me to this day.

Chapter 13

Stereotyping by Neurotypical Individuals

This is the only hurdle that is located outside of the bodies and brains of individuals with ASD. Thus, understanding and creating interventions concerning this hurdle remains the primary responsibility of all of us who know and/or work with individuals with ASD throughout their life span. All the other hurdles require that parents and professionals intervene intensively while individuals are infants, toddlers, and youngsters. As young people grow, however, it is important to educate them and teach them to both understand and advocate for their own needs. We want to teach people with ASD how these hurdles affect their lives, but the primary responsibility of educating and changing the dominant culture rests with all of us.

When neurotypical individuals interact with children and teens with ASD, we generally make four assumptions that cause difficulty and stress:

This youngster is being stubborn and controlling. We need to demand compliance in order to show we are in charge.
This assumption is grounded in the way that parents and teachers have been trained to deal with headstrong and dominating children. This is generally the response that mental health professionals will recommend when parents come to talk to them about children who will not follow limits and directions. When parents have difficulty setting and keeping limits, children can learn to enjoy the feeling of power as they discover that they have developed some elements of

control over their lives. Work then needs to be done to restore power to the parents.

Thus, this assumption is based on the belief that children have come to enjoy their power, and that adults need to reassert who is in charge.

As we learned in Chapter 5, this is not the motivation of children with ASD. Children with ASD, because they do not understand the world around them, feel their life is out of control, so attempting to wrest "power" away from them most likely will lead them to feel panicked. And, once panicked, they clearly come out of their band of regulation, and are not capable of learning. A different intervention is required – one not based on the assumption that the behavior is stubborn and controlling.

This child is so smart that learning what we are teaching should be easy.
Children with ASD can have an extremely uneven cognitive ability profile. Very often they can do some tasks very well, while having significant struggles with others. Many individuals have cognitive profiles in which they might be better in math than in reading, or science rather than social studies. But in children with ASD, this phenomenon can be much more pronounced. Thus we will have youngsters who are what I call "power-readers". They have memorized an extensive number of words, and can read material many years above their grade level. However, they cannot comprehend the material that they read. These young people will read a passage aloud in a way that will convince the adult that they are brilliant, but be unable to understand anything they have read. Similarly, many young students with ASD can memorize math facts (addition, subtraction, multiplication, and division) with ease, but cannot understand how to apply these, so that doing word problems is extremely difficult.

In addition to these problems within academic disciplines, many parents and teachers have difficulty understanding how a child who can read well cannot do math or write at even a basic level. Generalizing that because a student with ASD can do one or two skills with ease indicates that they should be able to learn anything with the same ease can create significant difficulties for the student.

This child is too cognitively impaired to be able to learn anything well.
This is the misconception that has provided me with the most challenge. I discovered that I hold this stereotype accidentally, and even today I have to challenge myself to make sure that I am not making this assumption.

The personal discovery came to me as part of the *FunJoyment* groups that are described in Part III of this book. As part of trying to create real social connections to classmates, I invite neurotypical students out of the classrooms of my students with ASD to be part of the group activities. In order to make sure that those students enjoy the groups, I developed a number of games and activities that have both intellectual and physical challenge. One of the games the reader will learn about is called *Big Dice* (see page 161). Big Dice is a game I invented that involves posting 9–12 pictures of common objects and animals on a metal whiteboard. A large die is then created allowing that die to be tossed on the floor in order to reveal one of four colors.[1] When the game starts, four pieces of colored poster board (corresponding to the colors on the die) are used to "hide" four of the pictures. In turn, each player rolls the die and attempts to remember what is "hidden" under the colored poster piece.

I am very often stunned while playing this game to discover that individuals who seem to lack rudimentary attention and memory skills can, and often do, memorize the entire board and become the expert consultant to the rest of the group. When this happens, I am humbled, but I also talk to the classroom teacher and begin to set up as many situations (including play time in the classroom) for this game to be played with many neurotypical peers. The neurotypical peers are amazed to discover this gift within their classmate, and many for the first time begin to look at the ASD student as a peer with unique gifts and skills.

Because an individual with ASD showed no interest/ability in an activity when it was introduced, they will never become interested.
This is an interesting stereotype, because I think very few teachers and parents would make this assumption about neurotypical children, but

---

[1]   With my youngest groups I have discovered that four colors (or sometimes even three) allow for enough success in the game. As students develop skills, the game can be made more challenging by the introduction of a six-color die.

this is a frequent misconception about a youth with ASD. I believe that this occurs because children and youths might not show an interest in an activity during the time frame that interest often blossoms within the neurotypical population, and adults can think the lack of interest/ability will now be lifelong. However, if we once again conceptualize that we are dealing with a delay in the development of neuropathways, interest and ability can come later. Many of the youngsters I know developed a delayed interest in reading fiction, playing a musical instrument, playing a physical game such as bocce ball, biking, and driving a car. We need to remember to keep reintroducing in order to see if there will be some "late blooming".

There is one other common and very disheartening stereotype that is having a negative effect on late teens and young adults with ASD. Employers and employees in the workplace may hold this one.

Individuals with ASD are definitely quirky, and present themselves with atypical interaction skills on the job. They can be labeled as "weird", "strange", "dorky", or "geeky", and be singled out for ridicule. The worst story I heard about this was a young man who spoke at an annual conference of the Autism Society of Minnesota. This young man was unusual in that he had very good gross motor skills and had learned to play tennis at a very high level while in high school. He did so well that his coach offered him a job teaching tennis to youngsters at a private country club. There he struggled mightily – his fine motor skills were so delayed that he could not properly chalk the lines on the clay courts, and he could not multitask to teach the children. He would become engrossed in teaching one or two and lose track of the others – sometimes they would simply wander off.

Instead of helping him, his coach berated and belittled him. The culmination of the abuse was the day the coach enlisted the help of the youngsters in a prank to lock the young man in the restroom. The man and children stood outside and laughed as the young man struggled to free himself.

This attitude – obviously not always taken to this extreme – is unfortunately embedded in our culture. Our young people are too often mocked and ridiculed by supervisors, instead of assisted. The supervisors who should be mentoring are joining or leading the abusing.

This is not occurring out of malice but out of ignorance. They simply do not understand our fine young people. Intervening in order to change this stereotype will largely be up to us – parents, teachers, and mental health professionals who understand individuals with ASD and honor their abilities and talents. We must be constantly ready to educate the people in our lives – at work, at church, at our clubs and organizations – until we have made the work world a welcoming place for individuals with ASD.

Chapter 14

Motivational Deficits

This hurdle should really not be any surprise, but it is amazing to me how casually so many adults can make the statement "He could do it, but he is so unmotivated". When I hear this, I want to grab people, shake them, and say, "And just how motivated are you to do things that are difficult – particularly when you are often surrounded by people who are doing things more easily than you?"

Think about it. We have just discussed nine significant hurdles that individuals face. Some neurotypical individuals face one or two of those hurdles, and they can have difficulty staying motivated. Imagine being an intelligent, inquisitive learner in a class or in any other learning situation. Around you are people with the same or sometimes less cognitive ability, *and they are doing tasks with relative ease.*

Here's a challenge – instead of imagining it, take a moment to think about types of learning that truly challenge you. How motivated are you to continue trying?

For me, the learning challenge I think about is learning to play chess. I have always been fascinated by the game. When I was young, the fact that it was so old and had all the romantic references to combat captured my young imagination. I would watch people playing chess, or look at chessboards on display at stores, and dream of being a Knight of the Round Table.

My parents bought my brothers and me a beginner set, and we played a bit. But I never mastered the moves, and never played it seriously. Even though I did not play often or well, I knew that the game was for really intelligent people. I thought of myself as really intelligent.[1]

Years passed. I devoted myself to finishing my degree work and starting a family. I worked for a school system, which meant that in the summer I had a lot of time off and not much money to spend. In the early 1980s, the school district began to get Apple II computers for classrooms, and encouraged staff to take computers home over the summer in order to gain skills using them. One summer I brought a computer home, and brought discs with learning games for my young children, and, for me, discs with keyboarding skills and chess.

I played chess against the computer approximately twice a day. The program could be set on beginner (I think that meant the computer would think two or three moves ahead), and I kept the setting on beginner all summer. I studied the moves that the computer made. I went to the library and took out books on chess strategy for beginners. I stayed focused and motivated.

At the end of the summer, the score was:

Computer 175 wins
John 0 wins
Draws 3

I have never played chess again. I break into a cold sweat when I think about playing it. My motivation is so low that if I am with a client and that young person wants to play chess, I actually decline. I cannot bring myself to face the board.[2]

There are many examples of young people who have become so discouraged that they refuse to attempt tasks. Because these examples abound, I do not use an example of a motivation problem in my video

---

1   I was fooled by the illusion in school that the brightest students got the best grades. I was reasonably intelligent, but I was blessed with great study skills, good organization skills, and good writing skills. This led me to get assignments done well and handed in on time. Getting the assignments done on time led to high marks, and in high school, I was ranked at the head of my class. I then took calculus. I studied and worked as hard as I could, but I could not get my mind around the concepts. I looked around the room and saw a handful of individuals breezing through the work and enjoying the challenge. These were classmates that had generally gotten lower final grades than me. At that moment I realized that they were really brilliant, that they would move on to great things in math and science. I was talented in getting tasks done. They were truly gifted.

2   In case you are interested and noted that I brought home a keyboarding disc, I was highly successful in teaching myself to type – which has resulted in, among other accomplishments, this book.

presentations. The example I use is one of truly remarkable motivation. I use it because of what it teaches us.

My colleagues were doing a videotaped assessment of Billy, and were getting fine evidence of the challenges Billy faces. At one point, a psychologist was trying to learn about Billy's ability to read situations and feelings based on viewing drawings. She was showing Billy the Roberts Apperception Test for Children cards, but was having difficulty trying to get Billy to discuss the pictures because he kept associating the situation in the drawings to his favorite themes of *Star Wars* and *Lord of the Rings*. Every time Billy looked at a card, he was responding with a scene from one of the movies.

In a final attempt, the psychologist prepared to show Billy one last picture, but first carefully set the stage by clearly asking him to respond as if the people depicted were ordinary folks – friends and neighbors – and not movie characters. In doing this careful preparation, she failed to notice that she was holding the card, and preparing to display it, upside down.

So, after making her expectations very clear, she held up a card depicting two seated adults and two standing children, all with serious expressions on their faces.[3]

Billy studied the upside-down card for about a half a minute, and the first statement he makes is, "Well, I don't really see how this card could have anything to do with *Star Wars* or *Lord of the Rings*."

He then further studied the card, and tilted his head slightly to get a better angle on it. Finally, he begins his description: "This is a family – a mother, father, and children. And the children are listening to their parents discuss...discuss about...discuss about how their world got turned upside down."

Now, Billy's ability to interpret facial and body expressions is seriously delayed, but my colleague's is not. This is an immediate clue to her. She checked the card and immediately turned it right side up. Billy studied the card a bit, and continued his description:

"And now the children are watching...watching their parents discuss... how their world got turned back over again."

---

3   The most typical response to this card is that this is a family, the children have gotten into trouble, and the parents are deciding what the punishment will be. Another common response is that the parents are divorcing and are announcing that fact to their children.

This is a remarkable piece of videotape. This was a young man who faced many hurdles, but who seemed completely nonplussed in the face of being asked to do something that was obviously very difficult for him. The adults in Billy's life – his parents, relatives, teachers, and other professionals – had obviously been very careful not to be judgmental with him. He had not faced significant criticism or had the relative skills of peers repeatedly pointed out to him. He was going to try his best, even though his best represented a significant delay when he was compared to same-age neurotypical peers.

I think about this often when I work with my clients, and when I hear parents and professionals complain that some are "unmotivated". Often the term is used as if it is describing a personality characteristic that cannot be influenced or changed.

But this is not the case. We all have a role to play in helping individuals facing hurdles and other learning challenges to stay motivated and maintaining effort. Teachers and professionals need to think carefully about the role they play in praising students who are organized and get work in on time in front of the whole class. I know from personal experience that such praise motivated me to continue to build on my academic strengths. What I am not sure of is the effect such praise had on students with less organizational ability. Did they become more motivated? Or did they become discouraged because they compared themselves to me and knew they were not able to compete with me?

I suspect it was the second. Because of this I encourage all teachers and professionals to praise in much more private ways and to measure each student against himself. Billy has something to teach all of us about staying motivated in the face of significant hurdles – but he is reaching a very small audience. The rest of us need to learn and pass on this knowledge.

Part III

FunJoyment Groups

Chapter 15

Introduction to FunJoyment Groups

FunJoyment groups are interventions that have been developed based on understanding the hurdles that challenge young people with ASD. The groups are designed to support and maintain the participants so that they can remain within their band of regulation. There are school-based groups developed for students in kindergarten through high school. In addition, there are community-based groups for youngsters from ten to 23 years old.[1]

The structure of the groups will be described in the following chapters. Following those chapters will be a description of all the games and activities used in sessions, information about how to make or purchase the materials, and hints about how to make the groups challenging and successful with the various age groups.

Although the sessions will be presented as appropriate for an age range, that range is appropriate for individuals with what would be described as Asperger's syndrome or high-functioning autism. Individuals who are more challenged with autism often become ready to successfully experience the social interaction in the group at a higher age. I have done the groups I will describe as appropriate for five- and six-year-olds with children aged ten and eleven. When I do that, I often train neurotypical ten- and eleven-year-olds to come to the group. This is a great way for typical youngsters to learn how they

---

1   I anticipate that we will continue to expand this age range. When I began community-based groups five years ago, we had nothing for young people after high school (18 years old). We developed the young adult groups in response to the desire of participants to remain involved. It is possible that in five years we will be running groups for individuals aged 25 to 30.

can successfully socialize with some of their peers with significant challenges, and helps introduce the young people to the possibility of a career in teaching or one of the helping professions.

Chapter 16

Concepts Important in All Groups

Although the groups are structured differently based on the age of the participants and whether the group is school- or community-based, there are some key concepts that remain the same in each group.

1. Getting ready

Doing groups with children and teens with ASD presents a rich opportunity for leaders to experience the hurdles, and multiple opportunities to observe behaviors and then create intervention strategies. Because so much can happen, group leaders should try to maximize positive reinforcement while minimizing the possibility of reinforcing a behavior that is not prosocial. In order to do this, I always recommend that these groups be co-led.[1] Co-leading allows group leaders to be able to:

1. observe every student in the group

2. make eye contact with each other and with group members – this allows non-verbal communication between adults and with the students

3. leave the room in order to help a student who has become unregulated while allowing the group to continue

---

[1] I have co-led groups together with social workers, psychologists, special education teachers, speech/language therapists, paraprofessionals, interns, and volunteers. Often, the combination of me working with a speech/language therapist has resulted in a dynamic partnership. Speech/language therapists are outstanding at providing the visual and auditory supports that allow students to make progress in interaction skills.

School-based groups have two leaders. Community-based groups usually have three leaders.

4. maximize opportunities to positively reinforce students who maintain themselves within their band of regulation when another student is struggling

5. discuss and plan for future groups based on multiple points of view

6. laugh, have fun, and engage the students in the fun.

Please note: Even though I developed these groups and have been doing them for 20 years, I try to never do a group alone. If a school district or organization does not provide me with a co-leader, I bring one of the paraprofessionals I have trained to the sessions.

Over the years, I have learned that preparation for the groups is vital to their success. What I have learned, through my own mistakes, is that preparing an environment that enhances the likelihood that students will be able to stay within their band of regulation is the most important factor in success. With that in mind, we will take some time to go through the elements that are necessary for that success, and the mistakes I made along the way that helped me learn.

Space

A specific space should be devoted to these groups. As my success grew in doing these groups in school settings, I was able to negotiate for an office space large enough to do groups. In the community, I rent or lease spaces from community businesses or service agencies. Generally, younger children have the most difficulty adapting to a space, but it is important to remember that these factors will influence the band of regulation of older participants as well.[2] The space should be:

- *Consistent* – Any new space can trigger the need for youngsters with ASD either to explore that environment, or to flee from the environment. I have led summer school groups for a school district for the last five years, so I often see the same students every summer. That district rotates the school it uses for summer school each year. Every year, even though the students:

---

2   When I needed to add a young adult group to my services because my teens were growing up, I had to move that group from an exciting coffee house to a staid large meeting room. The initial participants were upset, and some quit the program. Now that we are running, many participants report they prefer the new space.

- know me and my co-leader

- are familiar with the way I will set up the room for the group

- see the same whiteboard and posters,

the first day of summer group is filled with many meltdowns, individuals leaving for breaks, and off-task behaviors. At first I thought I was "rusty" in my skills in understanding and dealing with the students. But now I recognize that even with all the familiarity that we bring to the group, the fact that the group is meeting in a new space causes many of the students to become unregulated. It is important to understand that this will happen, plan for it, and, most importantly, not blame the students.

- *Dedicated to the group(s)* – Although I would obviously use my office for other purposes during the school day, I would try not to bring the youngest students with ASD into my room for any other purpose. It is difficult for young children to maintain their regulation state, and any confusion about what might be expected in a particular space adds to the difficulty. I learned this in a very humbling fashion. I had been leading a kindergarten group with two students with autism and four neurotypical peers. The group had been very successful and the students with autism were demonstrating social competence (within the limited skills that they were asked to do) to their peers. One day the principal asked to "borrow" my office to meet with a group of parents, and I generously agreed and moved my group into one of the special education classrooms. This was a huge mistake. One of the students with autism had a complete meltdown when he entered the classroom and saw me, the usual semicircle of chairs, the whiteboard, and the usual props. He yelled, screamed, hit, spit, and made it very clear that social group was not allowed in that classroom. And he did all of this in front of the neurotypical peers. I quickly walked the other students back to their classroom, and explained to them that I had made a terrible mistake. I learned my lesson. From that point on, I tried hard not ever to give up my space. If my office was not available, I canceled groups instead of moving them.

- *Safe* – Believe it or not, I'm talking mainly about chairs. Young students with cognitive developmental delays need to be sitting in chairs that allow them to place their feet firmly on the ground. I have, unfortunately, experienced students who become so excited and engaged, that they have literally fallen off chairs to the ground because they were unable to plant their feet firmly underneath them. Obviously, care should be taken to put away any sharp objects, as well as any substances that could be ingested, no matter what the age of the participants.

Consistent group leaders

The group leaders need to be consistent. A new person who doesn't know the routine can present challenges to the group. The students with ASD can become focused on:

- needing to know why there is a new person (substitute leader) in the room

- needing to explain every rule/expectation to that substitute

- pointing out every difference or "mistake" that person makes.

Of course, illnesses and schedule conflicts occur, and so inevitably there will be times when a substitute leader is present. On these occasions, it is usually very helpful to have a Social Story[3] ready to be reviewed with students either before they walk to group, or reviewed as soon as they sit down.

Important: Early in my experience, I thought it would be logical to use other adults who the students with ASD were already familiar and comfortable with as substitutes in the school groups. I tried using classroom paraprofessionals, special education teachers, nurses, principals, and even parents as substitute leaders. The results were almost always negative – sometimes very negative. The students would experience that person as an individual who is not in the "correct place" or doing the "correct" interactions, and would become upset and unregulated. This was a mistake I made many times before

---

3   Social Stories[TM] are a concept developed by Carol Gray. In brief, they are a pictorial or written visual support that explains the need for the change, and the feelings that result, and the strategies that will be utilized to help the student stay organized and regulated through the change.

I finally realized what was happening. Please learn from my error. It is almost always better to use a substitute teacher than use a familiar person in an unfamiliar role.

Consistent group schedule

My groups usually were scheduled to occur once per week at a specific time and day. Sometimes field trips and special events caused the students to be unavailable at group time. Again, early in the development of these groups, cooperative classroom teachers would sometimes generously offer to make the students available on a different day or different time. Once again, I learned that most often this was a mistake. The students with ASD found it very disorienting to have their routine changed – even for a group they very much enjoyed. Coming at a rescheduled time risked students demonstrating their rigidity and difficulty regulating themselves in front of neurotypical peers. I learned it is usually better to skip a group rather than reschedule a group.

So, the advice here in scheduling groups is to try to look ahead into the school or organization schedule, and try to schedule groups at times when there will be the least need to avoid conflicts.

Create a non-stimulating environment
SCHOOL GROUPS

Confession time. This concept was very difficult for me to accept. I ran into my own needs and my own rigidity.

As I explained above, I gradually learned that consistent space is important. I also learned that the space should be boring. There should be little to distract the students visually, and little to tempt them to explore through touch or smell.

Now, I am a trained therapist. For the other students that I saw, and parents I met, I wanted my office to be exciting, warm, inviting, and stimulating. I had pictures of my family and pets on the walls. I had bins of puppets and toys. I had stacks of games and activities. I had interesting lamps, mobiles hanging from the ceiling, building blocks, and readily available art materials. I had dazzling screensavers on my computers.

It all had to go. I was not happy. I was guilty of blaming the students. I had to go through the five stages of grieving as I transformed my inviting and cozy spaces into white-walled, boring, never-changing spaces. The shelves were replaced with cabinets and the cabinet doors stayed closed. My puppets and art materials went into opaque bins. My computer monitor had to be switched off during sessions. And, hardest of all, I had to learn to change my room radically every time I began a new activity. Before every session I would do a mad scramble to take out everything I would need and put away any distraction. When a parent came to see me, I had some warm and fuzzy materials I would display. If that parent brought a child with them, my puppets, blocks, and art materials needed to be out. Many days I felt more like a tech-crew member at a theater than a competent social worker.

But the results in the groups were huge and gratifying.

To this day, I love doing my sessions in my office. But I hate that I have a boring office.

COMMUNITY GROUPS

For my community groups, I try to have a quiet and non-stimulating location for the groups for ten- and eleven-year-old participants. However, I change that up significantly for teens. I currently use a coffee house for my young and older teen groups. As you will learn when these groups are discussed, we use the visual, auditory and olfactory distractions of this location to build up tolerances to enjoying activities while there are distractions. I see this as an important work skill, since many work environments have some types of distractions. However, we do meet in the same location week after week, so that the participants know the location of the doors and bathrooms, the comfort of the chairs, the types of drinks and treats available, and how to order and pay for their treats.

2. Peer group members

School groups

Although the groups can be done with only students with ASD – for example, in the summer school program I mentioned previously, there are no neurotypical students at the summer school, so using neurotypical students is not possible – these groups are most beneficial when neurotypical peers are included. Inclusion of neurotypical peers:[4]

---

4   Inclusion of neurotypical peers in a school setting requires the permission of their parents. Four sample letters that have been used when seeking the permission to include neurotypical peers can be found at the beginning of Part IV, *Materials and Activities*.

1. Creates the certainty that some students will always be focused and on task, allowing the leaders to comment on and positively reinforce those behaviors, instead of calling attention to (and negatively reinforcing) off-task behaviors.

2. Allows the neurotypical student to have meaningful interactions with the students with ASD.

3. Allows the neurotypical student to experience (most often for the first time) their classmates with ASD demonstrating social competence and confidence.

4. Presents the opportunity for relationships to be formed that might continue in the classroom, lunchroom, and playground.

5. Often creates an opportunity for neurotypical students who are shy, or lack some confidence, to practice social success.

6. Allows (through the recommended rotating of neurotypical group members every six sessions) many neurotypical students to experience their classmates with ASD in a setting in which they are more socially comfortable and competent than in the large classroom.

Community groups

Because community groups are fee-based, there are no neurotypical peers in the groups. I am able to create the positive examples of neurotypical peers by using group members in creative ways. Most of my clients stay in community groups for a significant length of time – many have been in one group or another for years.

I create volunteer experiences for my older teens to come and assist with the younger groups. Many teens are looking for volunteer experiences in order to fulfill requirements with their religious communities, and some schools give extra credit for volunteering in the community. For many of my clients, volunteering to help in groups is the first pre-vocational experience they have. Most are very successful.[5]

---

5   My daughter, Kelly Merges, has extended the volunteer possibilities by training many teens to be volunteer assistant coaches in the Challenger Division of the local Little League baseball program. The Challenger Division provides a baseball experience for youngsters with cognitive, developmental, mobility, vision, and hearing challenges. On Sundays in the summer, our teens can be found coaching children to play a game that they were not able to play because they had challenges and the league had not yet been developed.

3. Repetition

School groups

Group leaders are encouraged to begin with a few lessons (as little as six), and to repeat those lessons many times during the course of a school year. Remember, the emphasis on each skill is not actually the ability to use that skill. We are focused on the skills of enjoyment, and then the enjoyment of doing a favorite activity with friends. The actual core skill we are looking to develop is the ease and confidence necessary to succeed in a social interaction with same-age peers. We are trying to get the student with ASD to this point, and then for them to notice that:

1. they are having fun

2. they are competent in the tasks involved in having fun.

Each lesson takes time to learn, and then master. Learning is stressful, so remember that during the first, second, and even third sessions, the students with ASD might not be focusing on enjoyment skills – they will most likely be focusing on competence skills. As they begin to anticipate with delight the task of a group, they will be able to focus on the fun. You will be able to positively reinforce the fact that they are having fun. Groups become time for applause, high fives, and praise.

Community groups

Community groups are longer – 75 minutes for the ten- and eleven-year-old participants, 90 minutes for all the other groups. This requires that leaders have many more activities to do, but repetition is also important. New activities are introduced slowly, and leaders need to know that some participants will be interested in new games and activities, but most will shy away from a new experience. Once a game has been introduced and is enjoyed by some participants, the leaders gently support the individuals who are stressed by the novelty in learning a new skill. Mastery of the skill comes first. After that, we work on enjoying the experience of playing the game with a group of friends.

Chapter 17

School-Based Groups for Five-, Six-, and Seven-Year-Old Youngsters

QUICK SNAPSHOT

Number of leaders	Two – two professionals or one professional and one aide.
Number of participants	Six – could be all students with ASD; could have two or three neurotypical peers.
Location	Small group room – at least 12 feet x 12 feet.
Frequency	Once a week.
Length of sessions	20–25 minutes.
Necessary materials	• Small chairs • Metal whiteboard • Small desk or table.
Duration of group	Throughout school year – activities repeated in a cycle of 6–8 experiences.

Focal point of the group – the whiteboard and posters

The chairs are placed so that group sits in a semicircle facing a metal whiteboard.[1] The leaders sit at each end of the semicircle so each is observing the students across from them, and the leaders can easily communicate. The leader on the left-hand side is in charge of putting the reinforcement jewels up on the scoreboard. (Relax – the reinforcement jewels and the scoreboard will be explained a bit later.) For this reason, that leader will need to stay in that particular chair.

There will be times when the needs of the students change the placement of the second adult.

- Sometimes a particular student might need to sit by one of the leaders in order to better regulate.

- Sometimes that student might need to sit closest to the wall so that she is only next to an adult.

- At times wider spacing can be achieved by putting an extra chair or two in the semicircle. The leaders can then assign a child to a spot next to one or two empty spaces.

- An extra chair placed in the semicircle can also easily create the flexibility to move a student who is distracting or being distracted. These are all decisions the leaders make before the group begins.

But, regardless, the focal point is the whiteboard. The scoreboard is there, posters indicating steps in role-play are displayed there, and the board itself can be used to play games.

Whiteboards, scoreboards, and posters are:

- *Static* – Adult leaders like to be animated and expressive with their faces and bodies. These communications, however, are often the most difficult for students with ASD to comprehend.

---

1   The importance of a metal whiteboard is that magnets will stick to it. Having tried other methods of quickly placing posters and reward indicators on a display surface, nothing has worked as well as purchasing magnet tape or magnet dot stickers and attaching the magnets to the back of what you want to display.

　　If you do not have a permanently fixed whiteboard, or if your whiteboard is not metal, small (35" by 17") whiteboards are available at office supply stores. (I travel with three white boards in my car.)

Being asked to learn about body language and social fun at the same time is a very difficult task. So we focus on the fun.

- *Visual schedules for these young students* – They orient the student to what will happen next, and how long the group will be lasting. If a student loses focus or needs to leave the room for a break, he can easily refocus on the task by being oriented to the whiteboard.

- *Create a wrap-around comfort* – There is much within each session that is routine and comforting, and the whiteboard displays the visual evidence of this routine.

The scoreboard

We are now ready to start the session using our primary tool – the scoreboard. The scoreboard consists of four graphic depictions on a poster board or tag board. It is approximately four inches wide and 22 inches long.[2] The graphics are displayed vertically. The scoreboard has magnetic tape attached so it can easily and securely be placed on the whiteboard.

The leaders have magnetic objects to place on the scoreboard to indicate accomplishment. I use plastic jewels that I purchase at a local craft store, and to which I attach magnetic dots. I like the jewels because of their size (about a half an inch in diameter) and their colors. They come in seven colors – red, blue, green, purple, yellow, pink, and clear.

The scoreboard allows us to positively reinforce the behaviors we want to see, and creates enough routine in each session so that students with ASD are supported to stay within their band of regulation. They are then most likely to learn and to practice the skills and games. Perhaps more importantly, they learn and practice laughing and having fun.

After doing these sessions for a number of years, a speech/language intern, who was learning from my co-leader and me, made an observation. She pointed out that the scoreboard created such a ritual of beginning and ending that there was most often only about 15 minutes of time spent on the daily task. Thinking this might be a

---

2   Directions for making the scoreboard are included in Part IV, *Activities and Materials.*

problem, my partner and I began to experiment with ways to speed through or eliminate those elements. The results were distressing. Students could not stay regulated because they were not finding the session predictable (and thus comforting) enough.

Note: One huge difference between the groups for these young students and the groups for older students is this dependence on the scoreboard ritual. Older students are weaned away from this dependence, and given other, less static visual supports.

Ready to start

When the students and I enter the office, I sit, tap the top graphic, and say, "I'm looking for students who are ready to start."

I immediately begin to name the students who are sitting, and ask them what color jewel they want. They reply and we begin to create a line of jewels to the right of the graphic.

Some students will take time to settle into a chair. Many times they will ask for a jewel. I remind them that I will call on them for a color when they are sitting. When they sit, I may call on them immediately (if I believe they need immediate reinforcement), or call on a student or two before them (if they are working on short delays of gratification). If a student gets up and wanders away after getting a jewel, I will slide it out of line with a promise that it will be slid back when the student returns, but I never take a jewel down. If a student gets up, stands at or behind his chair (but stays oriented to the task), I will leave the jewel and explain to the other students something like, "Billy learns best while standing, so for him it is okay to stand." Each participant picks a jewel for being ready to start – even the adult leaders.

- For some students, picking out one color from seven choices is overwhelming. When I believe this is happening, I will put two different colored jewels in my hand, display them to the student, and ask that one be picked.

- Some students have such a delay in speech, or such significant motor planning issues, that they struggle to get the single word out. In these cases I will display some jewels in the palm of my hand and let the student select one by pointing at it.

Many students quickly become comfortable with the format, and the *Ready to start* ritual can be extended to include more learning and more fun. Recommendations are:

1. *Asking an individual student to identify who is ready to start.* It is best to begin with neurotypical students when moving to this stage. They will model the skills. This is a really important stage for the group process. We most often find that the students with ASD do not know many classmates by name – even though they may have been in class with them for weeks or months. This is a great way for ASD students to gently and proficiently learn the names of their peers.

2. *Create patterns with the colors* – for example, red, red, blue; red, red, blue, etc. Students like the patterning and will often communicate to one another what they want to see. I always express delight when a pattern is extended, and I also express delight when an individual breaks the pattern and starts something new. Do not be rigid about the fun – try to find the enjoyment in any group interaction.

3. *Change the color names to flavors.* Red becomes cherry, raspberry, or strawberry; green becomes lime or grape. But wait, grapes can be green, red or purple, leading to, "Is it a red, purple or green grape?" Laugh a lot, and be creative.

Compliments – making people smile

There is perhaps no social interaction as common or as consistently positive as the ritual of "I like your _____" or "I like you because _____", followed by "Thank you" and "You're welcome". But, although it is very common, it involves both the ability to see and appreciate something about another person, and the ease, comfort, and confidence in stating it. Following this comes the smile that a compliment evokes and the pride in oneself after giving a compliment. For this reason – the fact that giving and receiving a compliment consistently brings joy into our lives – I make compliments a part of every session.

So, once we are all ready to go (or as close to that as I think we are able to achieve), I begin the ritual of giving and receiving a compliment. Initially, the adults go first. The process is:

1. Identify the person you are giving the compliment to by name.

2. Make eye contact.

3. State the name first, and give the compliment. For example: "Jimmy, I like your blue and red tee-shirt." (I reinforce the stating of the name first. After lots of experience of children giving a compliment and using the name last – as in "I like your tee-shirt, Jimmy" – I realized the recipient of the compliment was often not paying attention until they heard their name. The most common response then was "What?" – leading to the need to repeat the statement. Thus the gentle reinforcement of a prosocial conversation skill – stating the name of the person you are talking to first.)

Following the compliment and the responses, the person who gave the compliment gets to pick the color for the jewel that will go on the line to the right of that graphic on the poster.

As both the students with ASD and the neurotypical students are learning this skill, there are a number of ways for the leaders to extend the learning. Young students often start with very basic compliments – "I like your shoes", "I like your pants", "I like your shirt", etc. Once there is comfort at this level, I like to model:

1. Using descriptors:

    "I like the dragon on your shirt."

    "I like the cool blue color of your pants."

    "I like those awesome new shoes."

2. Talking about actual characteristics and qualities of a person:

    "I like the way you wait patiently."

    "I like your smile."

    "I love the way you laugh."

    "I like the way you sit quietly."

Having demonstrated those skills, I gently begin to encourage the students to add descriptors to their statements, often by giving a direct example. Following the statement "Jane, I like your shirt", I might ask, "Do you like the color or do you like the picture?" Once the student has answered that question, I model the entire statement, "Jane, I like the Spiderman picture on your tee-shirt", and ask the student to repeat the whole statement. I find that neurotypical students, as well as students with ASD, benefit from opportunities to develop this skill.

Our least skilled group participants might need a lot of support in order to give a compliment successfully. For those students, I have the following recommendations:

1. If a student seems overwhelmed with the decision to pick out someone from the large group to receive the compliment, the leaders can suggest the choice of two possible recipients.

2. Once the student has decided whom to compliment, but is now struggling with the actual compliment, the leaders can suggest two possibilities. For example:

   "I like your haircut."

   "I like your smile."

3. If the student is still stuck, the leader can give the actual compliment and ask the student to repeat it.

Some students with limited language skills will be unable to speak a sentence longer than a few words. In those cases, a student should be reinforced for looking at the person and saying something as simple as "Nice shoes".

Additional important points to remember:

- Everyone (including the adults) should give a compliment.

- Everyone likes to get compliments, so keep track of who has received compliments and begin to direct the students to peers not chosen.

- Some students with ASD will get stuck giving the same compliment to the same person each group. The best way to nudge a student out of this pattern is to accept the ritualistic compliment, but then give the opportunity for a second compliment.

Being straight line

We are now ready for the planned activity for the day. (Suggested activities – games and role-plays – are in Part IV, *Materials and Activities*.)

All youngsters who have been part of preschool and school have heard language designed to indicate to them that they should pay attention. They have heard statements such as:

- Pay attention.

- Eyes front and mouths quiet.

- Freeze and listen.

- I'm looking for good listeners.

Soon after I began these groups, I realized that some students with ASD had developed dramatic responses (screaming, putting hands over their ears, shouting "No, no, no!", and even tantrums) to some of those commands, and that those responses would look very odd to neurotypical peers. So, I decided to invent my own language for this skill. The graphic depicts:

- a straight line, which represents anything I want to see – looking at a poster, sitting and waiting, raising hands, participating in the game or role-play, etc.

- a squiggly line, which represents any behavior I don't want to see. (Because I don't want to see it, it is crossed out.)

As we begin every activity, I explain what is *straight line* behavior. For these behaviors I will put up jewels. If there are behaviors that I don't want to see, I will comment that those are not *straight line* behaviors, and promise I will place jewels when I see the desired behaviors.

This has thus far allowed me to avoid bringing any ritualized reactions into groups, while allowing me to make my point about the behaviors I want to reinforce.

While the students are doing the activities, I keep them oriented and focused on the behaviors I want to see by placing jewels on a line to the right of the straight line and/or directly by the steps in the visual script for the role-plays. Information about what is to be reinforced is included in the descriptions of each activity in Part IV *Materials and Activities*.

A goal for the adults is to use this part of the scoreboard to reinforce the behaviors and interactions that are seen as positive and prosocial. I consider a perfect session one at which I never have to say "Stop" or "Don't". My concern is that children with ASD often have good sense for when they have gotten an adult's attention, but a poor sense of whether they are receiving positive or negative attention. My observation is that they may be reacting more to the fact that something exciting and energizing is occurring. Thus negative attention often provides significant reinforcement for a behavior. Basically, I have discovered that the more I say "Stop" or "Don't", the more I end up saying "Stop" and "Don't".

If a child loses focus, begins to talk or sing, or gets up and leaves the circle, my first move is always to positively reinforce with jewels the children who are focused, who are quiet, and who are in their chairs. Quite often this action alone will bring the child back to the desired behavior. But sometimes it does not. When that happens, my approach is to keep posting jewels and paying attention to the students who *are* being *straight line*. If I can keep the rest of the students focused, I am not concerned about the one who is off task. I continue the group while simultaneously observing the student who has drifted, and trying to determine which hurdle(s) might be in play. I will not say "Stop" or "Don't" unless other children join the student who has drifted.

I once did four weekly sessions with one student sitting under my desk humming. Toward the end of the fourth session, the student wandered over to the chairs and sat down. I immediately gave him a jewel for being *straight line*, and kept giving jewels about once per minute while he stayed in the circle. In about three weeks the humming under my desk disappeared.

Praising yourself

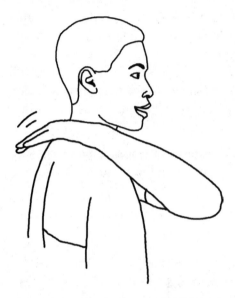

The session then moves close to conclusion with another ritual promoting a very important social interaction skill – praising yourself for what you have done. The ritual is very close to the compliment one. We take turns identifying that we are ready to "compliment ourselves", and do so with a complete sentence.

I like the students to be able to state an entire sentence beginning with:

"I did a good/great job today _____". Once more the adults go first to model possibilities. Again we choose the color jewel we want as reinforcement to be placed along side the graphic of the person "patting himself on the back". The supports for the students in this section of the group are similar to those used to help with complimenting:

- If a student has difficulty thinking about something she has done well, the adults will give two suggestions.

- Sometimes a student has had a "bad day" and has hardly participated at all. It is important for the leaders to point out something that was done well – even sitting quietly for a short time – and for this to be noticed and reinforced.

- Sometimes a child will pick out a negative skill to highlight. Some students have said, "I did a good job teasing Billy" or "I did a good job picking my nose". These students are told that we don't get a jewel for doing those things, but immediately asked if they want to praise themselves for some specific positive behavior that I noticed during the session. Sometimes they will decline, and the process just moves to the next person. After a few weeks, almost every student will begin to make a positive comment because he wants the jewel.

- Once again students with expressive language problems need help either shortening or modifying the statement so they can be successful.

Counting the jewels

At the end of session, the students all want to count up the jewels and find out how high the score was for the day. The score is always what the entire group earned – no attempt is ever made to give anyone an individual score. I like to point to each jewel as we count together. I also choose to count each line of jewels from left to right and from top to bottom, thus mimicking the way our eyes move when we are reading. In order to add variety, I will often:

- stop the count and ask the boys to continue

- stop the count and ask the girls to continue

- stop the count and ask the kids to continue

- stop the count and ask the adults to continue.

Doing this adds to the fun and promotes attending to both the visual task and the verbal direction.

Finally, I will often ask the second graders to count by twos. (After all, they are in second grade.) I always present them with this visual map when I do so:

$$\_2, \_ 4, \_6, \_8, \_0^3$$

and I point to each position in succession in order to help the students with ASD visualize and understand the pattern.

Okay – now you are ready to try some sessions. The *Materials and Activities* in Part IV will give you specific activities and the materials you will need to get started. Look in that section for:

- permission letters

- scoreboard (and directions)

- activities and role-plays:

  o *Big Dice Game*

  o *Ask to Play*

  o *Charades*

  o *Ask for Help*

  o *Ask to Share*

  o *Interrupting an Adult*

  o *Bean Bag Toss*

---

3   I use this map as a way to visually depict the pattern involved in counting by twos. The first time I point to the sequence, we recite: 2, 4, 6, 8, 10; the second time through, we recite: 12, 14, 16, 18, 20; the third time through, we recite: 22, 24, 26, 28, 30; etc.

Chapter 18

School-Based Groups for Seven- through Eleven-Year-Old Youngsters

QUICK SNAPSHOT

Number of leaders	Two – two professionals or one professional and one aide. (A very experienced leader can lead this group alone.)
Number of participants	Six – could be all students with ASD; could have two or three neurotypical peers.
Location	Small group room – at least 12 feet x 12 feet.
Frequency	Once a week.
Length of sessions	30 minutes.
Necessary materials	• Medium-size chairs • Metal whiteboard • Round or octagonal table (large enough for the eight participants, small enough that the students can reach to the center in order to move game pieces).
Duration of group	Throughout school year – activities repeated in a cycle of 6–8 experiences.

Focal point of the session – the whiteboard

For this age group, the whiteboard continues to be the focal point, but it is blank as the participants enter the room. The chairs will be arranged in a semicircle if the activity is to focus on a conversation-based activity, and, if the activity is a board game, the chairs will be arranged around the table.

The whiteboard will serve the function of being:

- *A communication / clarification tool* – The three positive expectations for the day will be listed on the whiteboard.

- *A focal point for the end-of-session evaluation* – Each session will end with the group establishing a group score for their relative success with the day's activity. Some games and activities will make use of the whiteboard as part of the game.

- *A consistent ritual* – Each group will begin with referencing the three daily goals, and will end with evaluation.

Structure of the session

The three daily goals

Each session begins with the adult leaders announcing the activity of the day, and then immediately announcing (and writing) the three daily goals. The goals are always stated positively – once again a goal for the leaders is to try to complete each session without having to say, "Stop" or "Don't". In this group, the method the leaders use to reinforce the positive is by referring the group members to the posted goals.

During conversation activities, I generally stick to three goals. These are:

- *Wait for your turn to speak* – For the conversational activities in the *Activities and Materials* section, I help the students with this task by using a talking object – for example, a stick, wand, bean bag, small stuffed animal – that is passed around the circle. If you are holding the object, it is your turn to speak. If you do not have the object, it is your turn to listen. When children forget and impulsively speak, I tap the whiteboard by this goal as a reminder. If that does not work, I verbally repeat the goal.

- *Listen with your ears and with your eyes* – Most students with ASD have been told repeatedly to look at the teacher or speaker. Most have difficulty doing this, partly because of their relative difficulty in reading facial expressions and body language. Many of my students tell me they can listen to the words better if they do not look at the speaker. I acknowledge that this might be the case, but stress the point that when a person is speaking, it makes the speaker feel very nervous if listeners are not looking at them for a significant part of the time. I stress that looking at the speaker is a courtesy that makes the speaker feel good. I then go back to the whiteboard and draw an arrow to extend from the word eyes, and add the phrase "about half the time". I let the group know we will be trying to make each other feel good by looking at the speaker about half the time.

- *Make sure every opinion is treated as "okay"* – The two conversation activities provided both ask participants to express opinions. The fact that opinions are not "right" or "wrong" is stressed. We can disagree, but students are urged to make sure that every person feels respected – even if we disagree.

I also have an alternative goal that I use selectively when needed. A common characteristic of children with ASD is that they may like to talk at length about a topic that interests them. Quite often they are unskilled in picking up the cues that peers are not very interested in what is being discussed. Listeners may also be giving signals that they are either bored or annoyed. In social skills groups, students are taught to look for and correctly interpret the facial and body language that might indicate that listeners are becoming bored or annoyed.

Because *FunJoyment* groups focus on the skills of social enjoyment, I approach this concept from a slightly different angle. When I anticipate that I will have a student or two who may talk at great length, I substitute (or even add as a fourth) this goal:

- *Be brief*

I then explain that being brief means using only two or three sentences when it is our turn to speak. I explain that, since the fun in a conversation is getting many chances to talk, if we are all brief with our comments, everyone will get more time to talk, and everyone will have more fun.

During partner game activities, I have three basic goals:

- *Be "okay" with your teammate* – Teammates will be assigned randomly. I stress that learning to work with any person in the room is an essential work skill. We will all someday have a boss who will assign us to work on a task with a co-worker. At that time the boss will not ask (or even care) if the person is a good friend or someone with whom we might not get along well. The task is to get the job done. Today's task will be to have fun while working with a random teammate.[1] I always poke fun at myself and the other leader by stating that there needs to be no complaining when someone is stuck being our partners. Occasionally, it will be obvious that we do not want two students to be paired together. I then pre-plan a method that will allow me to manipulate the results, or tell the group that, in order to save time, I picked names out of a hat before group began.

- *Teammates must make decisions together* – This is crucially important, and the examples that the adults set in discussing possible moves and negotiating a result are vital to the students learning skills. I often have to coach my co-leaders to make sure they are occasionally forceful that their opinion needs to be considered – adults can have a tendency to model capitulation. If one team member is dominating a team, I temporarily halt the game and require a team consultation. If the team is really stuck, I teach a compromising skill on the spot. This is the crucial skill. It is more important than finishing the game. If the discussion slows the progress of the game, I always have ways of determining first, second, third and fourth winners at the end of the group.[2] I tell the students I never allow the L-word (loser) to be used in my room. This generally results in a focus on calling me a

---

1 I have various ways of randomly finding teams. Examples are: mixing up two of each color game pieces and dropping the pieces in the hands of the players, alphabetizing middle names, putting birthdates in order from January 1 to December 31, and putting the last four digits of our phone numbers in order of the smallest to the largest.

2 Methods for determining the sequence of winning teams is given in the adapted directions for the board games provided in *Activities and Materials* in Part IV.

loser, which I pretend to be greatly hurt to hear. That adds to the fun and helps keep the students from designating other students "losers".

- *Have fun no matter if you are first, second, third, or fourth winners* – This is basically teaching good sportspersonship and emphasizing fun over winning. I point out that our professional athletes, who pout, taunt, strut, and gesture, do a terrible job of being good sportspersons, and challenge the students in front of me to set an example for them.

I have some alternative goals that I will strategically use if I have some students having difficulties with game playing. These include:

- *Know when it is your team's turn* – I use this when students are struggling with either impulsivity or inattention. If a student is really struggling, I create a cardboard arrow that one of the leaders shifts so that it always points to the team playing at the moment, and/or prompt a team by directly telling them, "Your turn will be next."

- *Compromise with your teammate* – When a few group members are really struggling to reach decisions, I teach that a compromise is a way to meet in the middle, and then directly tell that team what a good compromise is if they are stuck. When an individual student is having great difficulty learning this skill, I manipulate the teams so that student is my partner. I then work diligently on explaining and re-explaining the skill of compromising.

- *Wait to help until asked* – I add this goal when playing the game *Pick It* with the adapted rules supplied in Part IV, *Activities and Materials*. In this game, players are encouraged to look at the cards displayed by other teams so they can help if a team thinks they are stuck. This is a terrific way to teach youngsters the fun of helping others, but to also wait while those teammates are thinking through their options.

- *Compliment others for their move or the way they treat teammates* – Just like the daily compliments in the young group, this reinforces the skill of saying something nice to another person. When I introduce this goal, I will often call a halt to group two or three times during the game or activity in order to prompt everyone to give one compliment. After doing this a few times, the compliments become much more natural and flow more easily into the course of the activity.

Evaluation

After every game and activity, the group members and adult leaders decide on a point value for the effort at meeting the three group goals. I use the following scale:

5 = Excellent

4 = Very good

3 = Okay

2 = Crummy, lousy, weak

1 = Mr. Merges cries.

I ask everyone (adults included) to think of a number that best represents how the *whole group* did on the goals. Once they have done that, I ask them to transfer that number to their closed fist, and finally, when everyone has done that, to open their hands to reveal their number. I ask that no one change their number in response to seeing the other numbers, since we value every opinion. Finally, I tell the group members that I expect them to be realistic, and that, if they are not, the adults can override the opinions of the group members.

We then open our hands, and reveal our numbers. Initially, the biggest issues are:

1. The perfectionists who either expect things to be perfect in order to get a five (I explain the difference between an excellent effort and a perfect result) or will come up with additional

reasons to downgrade the group (for example, "Billy burped and did not say excuse me")[3]

2. The students who are so motivated to hit the reward number that they signal a five no matter what has occurred during group.

Over the course of a few weeks, it appears to me that most students begin to try to predict how the adults evaluate, and begin to match the adults. I believe this is a very serviceable evaluation technique. It mirrors a kind of empathy and "mind reading" skill.

I believe that the skills learned in the evaluation process are among the most valuable learned in this group process.

The evaluation process ends with those who evaluated less than five being asked to talk about which specific goal could have been improved upon. This is also a valuable skill – learning to be able to articulate how a judgment is made. Over the course of many weeks, the students improve significantly in their skills in observing themselves and discuss their rationale.

There is one more event that may be encountered. Occasionally something happens during a session (or perhaps before a session) that leads a student to be out of her band of regulation during group time and perhaps do very poorly on all goals. When this happens I ask the group to evaluate as described above, and we generally reach a two or three point value. When we discuss why we are evaluating so low, inevitably the "bad day" that one person had is referenced. I allow this to happen, and then say, "You know, _____ has had a very bad day today. Something has really made her upset and grumpy. Well, we all can have bad days, and this might happen to any of us. So we won't take away group points due to one person having a bad day. Let's evaluate again, but this time consider the efforts of everyone except _____."

---

3   It is perhaps not surprising that one result of teaching essential social skills and rules are that some young people become the "rule police". I combat that tendency by acknowledging that they are correct about the social rule they are referring to. I then tap on the whiteboard and point out that we were not working that day on that social skill. I further point out that it is impossible to work on all rules and expectations all the time. This statement seems to greatly benefit those youngsters who have become rule-bound by memorizing every social skill they have been taught. Many students become visibly relaxed when they incorporate the idea that not every social rule has to apply importantly in every situation.

In doing this we accomplish two tasks. We let the student who struggled know that sometimes things are beyond her control, but we value her and don't want to blame her. We also let everyone know that no one will ever be able to sabotage a group by deliberately flouting the group goals.

Finally, the adults designate a number value for that day's session.

Group reward

The points accumulate toward a goal. I always make my goal 25 total points. When the group reaches that goal, I take them through a process I have developed that includes:[4]

- brainstorming

- compromising

- reaching a consensus.

My process is effective, but a bit complex. It took me a few years of tinkering to perfect, and it requires moving things along at a brisk pace and multitasking in order to accomplish in 30 minutes. I suggest that professionals new to the process experiment with ways to gather input, discuss, and then reach a decision that feels right to them. For anyone interested in my specific technique, please send me an email and I will send the information to you.

Earning the reward provides an opportunity for group members to set up a table, share a treat, talk while eating, and then clean up as they end their experience together. I suggest the leader ask questions that everyone will answer in turn (e.g. "What will you be doing over

---

4 Reaching the group goal leads me to my favorite story about a group. I was leading a fifth session at an elementary school with a group that consisted of two students with ASD and four neurotypical students. As we entered the fifth session, the group had accumulated 23 points. They were also having such a great time that they did not want the group to end. So they conspired to extend the group.

Knowing that if they made me cry, they would only get one point (and thus total 24 points), they proceeded through my activity at their usually high level. However, at the end of the group, when I turned my back on them in order to review the daily goals, one of then unzipped a plastic bag, tiptoed up to where I stood, and held the bag at about my eye level. When I turned back to face them, the essence of chopped onions flowed over my face, and tears streamed from my eyes.

They triumphantly pointed out that I had to give them one point because I was crying. I smiled my agreement through my tears, gave them a one, and the group had to meet one more time. It remains one of the best experiences of my life.

an upcoming holiday?") or perhaps go around the group, selecting each member in turn, and asking everyone else to give the person a compliment or identify a quality that person displays. Practicing this is a great experience for the students with ASD. In their upcoming work lives they will undoubtedly be at birthday, engagement, retirement, and other social gatherings, and be asked to say something about the honoree. Having this practice will help each approach this with greater ease.

Suggested activities

Conversation activities
- *Introductory Questions*
- *Question Cards*
- *A through Z game*
- *Evaluation process*

Game activities
- *Up the River*
- *Pick It*
- *Mr. M's Minefield*
- *Bean Bag Toss*

Chapter 19

School-Based Groups for Junior High and High School Students

QUICK SNAPSHOT

Number of leaders	Two – two professionals or one professional and one aide. (A very experienced leader can lead this group alone.)
Number of participants	Six to eight – could be all students with ASD; could have two, three, or four neurotypical peers.
Location	Small group room – at least 12 feet x 12 feet.
Frequency	Once a week.
Length of sessions	30 minutes.
Necessary materials	• Chairs • Metal whiteboard • Round or octagonal table (large enough for the eight participants, small enough that the students can reach to the center in order to move game pieces).
Duration of group	Throughout school year – activities repeated in a cycle of 6–8 experiences

Please review the following sections in the previous chapter. The information needed to lead these groups is the same. The groups will also:

- *Use the whiteboard as the focal point and communication support –* The whiteboard is used in exactly the same manner as in the younger group. It is the primary communication tool. The three daily goals are listed on the board. The leaders will tap the board to reorient anyone who has lost focus, and take a brief "time out" during the game or activity to go over goals verbally and visually should many participants in the group lose focus. Often, taking such a time out serves to remind the neurotypical peers why they are there, and to help them move to being the strong models the leader desires.

- *Have three daily goals –* Many of the games and activities used with the younger students can still be used here. While playing *Up the River,* leaders will note that both the ability to create a strategy and the ability to communicate that strategy to partners can be extended. While playing *Pick It,* partners with higher skills can be challenged to teach their partners how to approach making decisions. I have discovered that even high school students enjoy the challenge of *Bean Bag Toss –* especially when the distance from thrower to targets can be increased.

  The goals for conversation and team games can be phrased the same as those listed in the previous chapter. Leaders would then expect participants to demonstrate these skills at a level closer to that of teens. (The addition of neurotypical students as models increases the ease in demonstrating skills.) In addition, there will be a number of games introduced at this age that will be played as individuals. Suggested goals for games that involve participants taking turns leading the group[1] (use three) are:

  o listen while leader reads the phrase or question

  o make your decision quickly

  o give the judge time to think (for *Apples to Apples*)

---

1   Examples are *Apples to Apples, Imaginiff,* and *Smart Ass.* See Part IV, *Materials and Activities,* for information about how to adapt these games for use in groups.

o laugh a lot

o enjoy the game even when your answer is not picked/is not correct.

A number of card games can be introduced to this age group[2]. Suggested goals for these games are:

o pay attention – know when it is your turn

o be ready to play

o have fun no matter what happens.

- *Use the five-point evaluation system* – The evaluation using the five possible points is exactly the same as the younger group. The difference is in the nuances that the leader can bring to each of the point values. As students mature and gain experience with the point system, the leaders can model greater sophistication in consideration. Having enough time for each student to say a few sentences about how he reached a particular conclusion becomes an important part of the evaluation process. It is during the evaluation process that leaders will begin to see individuals incorporating phrases and even whole sentences that were heard previously into their explanations. The students will demonstrate increased flexibility and sophistication because they have added key phrases to their memory that will allow them to be able to explain their points of view.[3]

- *Provide a group reward* – Once again the group is rewarded for reaching a goal of 25 cumulative points, and the leader takes them through either a process of their own design (or my process[4]) that includes:

---

2   *Turnabout* and *Moose in the House* are suggested card games. Again, information about how to adapt these games is in Part IV, *Materials and Activities*.

3   Keep in mind the technique needed (and explained in the previous chapter) to use in case a particular student has a very bad day and is unable to stay within the band of regulation during the group. Giving that student honest feedback about the effect their behavior has had on individuals and the group process in the first evaluation is important. Re-evaluating gives the message to every group member that "a bad day" is understandable and able to be forgiven. It also diminishes the power of any misbehavior.

4   Again, if a leader is interested in my process, please send me an email and I will provide the details.

- brainstorming

- compromising

- consensus.

At this age (if the structure of the school can support creating the possibility that a group to get together one time for 12 weeks instead of seven), I have added the possibility of waiting until 50 points are earned and then providing a bigger reward. I use this technique with groups in which I have a number of participants (could be either students with ASD, neurotypical students, or both) who have been in groups before and understand the process. We begin the group by deciding what we are working for. My bigger rewards include:

- going out for lunch at a fast food restaurant

- having a pizza lunch delivered to the school

- bringing my Wii system in and playing group Wii games.

Once the group has decided the goal, the weekly groups become a countdown to the day when the reward is earned and the reward time can be scheduled.

Finally, during these older groups, the concept of playing games in which the group members are divided into two competing teams is introduced. This concept looks a lot like a television game show, with one leader being the host, and the other leader becoming a part of one of the teams. (It is a good idea to have the second leader join the team that will most likely have a more difficult time reaching a consensus.)

The leader who is "hosting" the game stands at the whiteboard and uses the board as the focal point, and also as the place where the host will *visually* list the information that has been *verbally* provided. This assists the students with ASD in two important ways. They:

- are assisted in holding the accumulated information in their minds

- have an easy way to reorient to the task and information in case they became distracted.

An extremely important function of the host is to reinforce that an answer is not an answer until the team reaches a consensus. Many times individual team members will impulsively shout out an idea. Even if the answer is correct, the host must remember to re-direct the discussion to the whole team. I use phrases such as "Does the whole team agree with that?" or "Is that the team's final answer?" in order to accomplish this. The "host" must keep in mind that the importance of the task is to develop the skills necessary to discuss and compromise as members of a group, not to get the correct answer. Many times during the playing of these group games, a quiet team member will suggest the correct answer but be overridden by louder, more assertive, teammates. An attentive host will see this happening and cue a team to begin to listen to the quieter teammate. In doing this, an important skill will be promoted in the assertive team members.

Suggested team games that are added to promote these skills are listed below. Instructions on how to adapt these games to fit the host format are listed in Part IV, *Activities and Materials*.

Suggested activities

Conversation activities
- *Introductory questions*
- *Question Cards*
- *A Through Z Game*
- *Evaluation process*

Game activities
- *Up the River*
- *Pick It*
- *Mr M's Minefield*
- *Bean Bag Toss*

Games played as individuals
- *Apples to Apples*[5]
- *Imaginiff*
- *Smart Ass*
- *Mr. M's Uno*

Two-team games
- *Twenty Questions*
- *Password*
- *Loaded Questions*
- *Sort It Out*
- *Bocce Ball* (weather permitting)

---

5   For students with cognitive delays, *Apples to Apples Junior* should be used.

Chapter 20

Notes About Community-Based Groups

The next chapters will describe specific elements of the community-based *FunJoyment* groups. There are, however, some basic tenets that run through all the groups. These are described below.

Open-ended groups

Open-ended (versus closed-ended) is a term I rarely hear anymore. When I first was trained in group work, this was a concept that was valued by group leaders. Basically, a closed-ended group is one in which all members begin and end on the same day. The experience begins on the first day, all members experience the same sequence of interactions, and all end on the same date. Today almost all community and school groups are closed-ended. The reason is simple: it is much easier to bill for a closed number of group sessions, and easy to cancel a group if enough participants do not enroll.

Open-ended groups allow (and even depend upon) participants enrolling in an ongoing fashion. Some participants are joining when others are leaving, or "graduating". The most common open-ended groups today are in-patient chemical dependency programs, and AA/Al-anon meetings.

The principal benefit of open-ended groups is the fact that these groups develop a culture over time, and, by adding members one at a time, the new members can very easily learn that culture. For example, my community-based groups have developed a very relaxed and honest atmosphere. Property is valued. Young people bring in iPods, laptop computers, and some favorite trading cards and game pieces.

Nothing has ever been damaged or stolen. They also bring money to buy treats, and sometimes leave change on the tables. Again nothing has ever been stolen. This cultural expectation is passed on (with little comment or explanation) to each new participant.

A second cultural element that has developed is ordering food and drink at the counter at the coffee house.[1] When we first began, participants did not order. It took many weeks and many interventions – introducing the counter staff to my group, taking participants one at a time to look over the food and drink items, and finally giving participants Depot bucks[2] – in order to establish comfort in purchasing at the counter. Today, as we enroll new members one at a time, a new participant might be shy about ordering for a week or two, but, by simply watching the other participants, usually begins to order within a few weeks.

A third cultural element passed on to new clients is the willingness to be interested in new games and experiences. New members are invited (by the current participants) to play or watch the play of games that are new to them. We also train participants to be coaches regarding their favorite games. Thus two types of important skills – teaching and learning – are being practiced within the groups.

The final part of group culture that is passed on is trust in the adult leaders. Just as in the school groups, the *FunJoyment* leaders are trained to consider a perfect group to be one in which the words "Don't" and "Stop" are never used. The teaching and coaching is very gentle – imbedded in the activities. Participants are never told they have to participate. If someone is having a bad day and wants to sit alone, we allow that. Leaders will periodically check in with someone who has separated herself, and usually the participant can be engaged in at least a two-person game with a leader. Again, the ease with which the leaders and participants interact is something that has developed over time. Now that it strongly exists, it is something that new participants learn to recognize quickly in their group experience.

---

1   My main groups meet at The Depot Coffee House in Hopkins, MN. This is a non-profit coffee house dedicated to being a safe, chemically free "hang out" for community teens.

2   We bought Depot bucks for each participant. These were coupons worth a dollar, but only at the Depot. With the incentive of free money, we got the most anxious of our participants to order at the counter.

For the reasons listed above, the most difficult aspect of a *FunJoyment* group is beginning a new group. New groups demand significant preparation and a rapid learning curve for the leaders. Remember, if the leaders are starting a new group, they are trying to learn about and develop relationships with between seven and nine young people at once. With open-ended groups, new relationships come along gradually.

In truth, for billing purposes, I do a modified open-ended group. By that I mean that participants can enter at any time, but once a young person becomes a member, I ask families to re-enroll for an entire course of sessions. (I offer four seasonal courses of sessions during the year – fall, winter, spring, and summer. Each lasts about eleven weeks, with one or two weeks between sessions, and some weeks off for holidays.)

Using this method, I have been able to both continue to create comfortable, safe environments and grow the program. I began with one group of seven junior high participants. That grew by word of mouth, and the participants aged. I soon had two groups – junior high and senior high. As the high school students graduated, we added a young adult group. As parents of younger students heard about the program, they requested the fifth and sixth grade group. Most young people enroll in the program and stay enrolled for years[3]. I have participants in my young adult group who began the program as junior high students.

Community locations

I have been fortunate in gaining access to highly desirable and comfortable community locations. We have been able to lease or been given access to marvelous spaces that the young people enjoy coming to, and, maybe more importantly, do not associate as being places where clinical assessment and treatment is occurring. The participants rarely talk about their *FunJoyment* group, but most often refer proudly to their group by the location name. They tell family and classmates

---

3   Frequently, parents will request that their child "drop out" of the program for a session, but ask me to hold a spot for their re-enrollment in the future sessions. Some reasons for the short "drop out" have been participation in a sport at school, being involved in a school play, academic tutoring, driver's education classes, employment, and, in one case, a foreign exchange opportunity.

about their Depot Group or their Pavilion Group. We encourage this. We also encourage participants to come to the group's location on days we are not meeting – just to hang out.

Parents meeting parents

This aspect of the groups ended up surprising me. I assumed that parents would be most interested in dropping off their children and having 90 minutes to run errands or have some time to themselves. Of course, many do. But the majority of the parents have created connections for themselves with other parents, and schedule days to meet to talk. Since participants come from many surrounding communities and school districts, the information they have shared has been invaluable to them. (Currently, seven moms of participants in the junior high group meet so regularly that I tease them that I am really running a day-care so that they can have a formal moms' group.)

I have learned to support this important element of the process by scheduling periodic half-hour parent meetings which occur during the groups. I step out of group to join them. During these times I try to make sure that new parents are introduced, and phone numbers and email addresses are exchanged.

Extending the experience

Getting to know so many young people and their parents has led us to a variety of ways to extend the group experience. My daughter, Kelly, who is a co-leader, coordinates the Challenger Division of the local Little League baseball program. The Challenger Division offers a modified baseball experience for players with physical, intellectual, and medical challenges. Many of our group participants have played in the program.

She has been very successful in training a number of junior high and senior high group members to be volunteer assistance coaches in the program. For most (if not all), this is their first volunteer employment. She has then become a work reference for them when they begin to apply for jobs.

Kelly has also worked out an agreement with a local card and game store to run Saturday afternoon games there, and to invite our participants to come and play the games they have learned in *FunJoyment* groups with peers from the surrounding community.

We have also trained high school and young adult group members to be volunteer leaders in the younger groups. This training is done with an eye on hiring them eventually to be paid co-leaders. We currently have one young adult who is paid to work in our weekly groups, and a number of volunteers working toward that status.

Lastly, our young adults have finally begun to plan a monthly outing for themselves. This was difficult – I believe because the act of having fun outside of group time with other group members seemed different enough to cause anxiety in most of the participants. They initially came up with many excuses. The first few gatherings were done with a lot of parent support, and were modeled to be similar to the group experience. Now they are more relaxed and have planned to attend some movies and meet for gatherings at individuals' houses. I am looking forwards to this gaining momentum and continuing to develop.

Chapter 21

Community-Based Groups for Ten- and Eleven-Year-Old Youngsters

QUICK SNAPSHOT

Number of leaders	Two – two professionals or one professional and one aide. I like to add a teen volunteer (a member of one of my community teen groups) to this as both a model and an additional resource.
Number of participants	Six to seven.
Location	Large group room – including an area to sit in a circle, an area to sit around a table, and an open space to do some large movement activities. Having a carpet on the floor is helpful (but not essential) in holding down the noise made by individuals and by chairs sliding across the floor.
Frequency	Once a week.
Length of sessions	75 minutes.

Necessary materials	• Chairs
	• Metal white board
	• One or two round or octagonal tables (large enough for the eight participants, small enough that the students can reach to the center in order to move game pieces).
	• Wii system (optional, but important)
Duration of group	Groups are scheduled throughout the year in ten/eleven weekly sessions.[1]

Moving these groups to a community location allows leaders to have extended time to help individuals with ASD learn social interaction/ social enjoyment skills. It also provides parents with a resource to assist their children's involvement in the community and in enjoyable games and interactions at a time when many students with ASD are meeting with some social obstacles. Once a child reaches ten or eleven years old, parents tell me that it becomes increasingly hard for them to schedule "play dates" with neurotypical neighbor peers and/or peers from school. This is due to a number of factors that begin to emerge at this age:

• Neurotypical youngsters begin to become less interested in particular activities, and more interested in conversation and spontaneity. These are skills that will develop later for young people with ASD.

• Many neurotypical youngsters are beginning to focus on particular skills – dance, theater, sports, etc. Again, the relative delay in the development of skills in young people with ASD creates a "skill gap" for many. In addition, success in a dance, theater, or sports group often depends on recognizing and learning many subtle social skills. Once again, students with ASD are relatively disadvantaged here by having only emerging skills.

---

1   I schedule my groups to coincide roughly with the seasons. I have a fall, winter, spring, and summer sessions.

- Typical ten- and eleven-year-olds are beginning to become very conscious of their social status, and concerned about "fitting in". Since individuals with ASD are in a minority, and untrained adults do not understand the disability, typical peers can begin to shy away from being willing to be seen interacting with a peer who is different, and perhaps considered odd.

Thus this stage of development can become a time when many children with ASD can begin to isolate themselves. They can retreat to the safety of their bedroom or basement, play with preferred toys, watch TV or favorite videos, and spend hours on the computer or playing video games.

Although doing the above is perfectly understandable – and we certainly want children to have fun – it is also very limiting. The limiting factor that is most concerning is that there is no opportunity to work on higher-level social interaction/social enjoyment skills, and thus no place to practice those skills so that they become a source of joy in the young person's life.

The number of participants in this group is kept deliberately low. Having only six or seven participants insures that they will have:

- many turns, thus helping them maintain interest and focus

- the support of an adult should they become unregulated or "stuck" in a situation

- fewer names of group member to learn (This is a surprisingly difficult skill. We make sure that we are constantly referring to group members by name, and asking them to do the same.).

Having a small number of participants helps leaders as well. Remember, the younger the participant, the more likely he is to slip out of the band of regulation. Adult leaders need to be observing carefully to learn the subtle signs that a participant is having difficulty with a hurdle, and be ready to support quickly and positively. More than any other community group, the fifth/sixth grade groups require the leaders to discuss their observations and plan carefully with each group. Little interventions, often no more than planning how to partner the youngsters during partner games (which need an adult partner; which combinations of two youngsters might lead one to become unregulated), the order of the activities in the sessions, and which participants need short breaks (e.g. a walk in the hall, a drink at the fountain) can be extremely important.

Structure

This group is based on a structure most similar to the one described in Chapter 17. Just as in that group, the focus of communicating what is happening during group is the whiteboard – not verbal communication. The major difference is that, with 75 minutes, the group will do three separate activities. That means that three times the whiteboard will be used to:

- identify the activity
- make explicit the three positive goals
- re-orient individuals (or even the whole group) if focus drifts
- score the activity using the five-point evaluation scale:

  5 = Excellent

  4 = Very good

  3 = Okay

  2 = Crummy, lousy, weak

  1 = Mr. Merges cries.

Just as in the school-based groups, there are some basic goals for conversation activities:

- wait for your turn to speak
- listen with your ears and with your eyes
- make sure every opinion is treated as "okay".

With the alternative:

- be brief.

With the team game activities, the goals are:

- be "okay" with your teammate

- teammates must make decisions together
- Have fun no matter if you are first, second, third, or fourth winners.

Alternative goals are:

- know when it is your team's turn
- compromise with your teammate
- wait to help until asked
- compliment others for their move or the way they treat teammates.[2]

At these community groups we also use games that are played as individuals. We do this with an eye on the reality that most of our participants will be moving on to our groups for teens, and also because, in life, many times we are playing games as individuals.

The most important skill to develop in individual-player games is the ability to have fun even if the person is not the winner. Over-focusing on winning is something often seen in early elementary-aged neurotypical peers. It should come as no surprise that, because of the relative developmental delay, our older elementary-aged participants are struggling with this. Parents often will identify this as a concern when enrolling participants. At home, they are often dealing with this behavior that has come to feel routine and even a ritual to their child. The *FunJoyment* group becomes a place to learn a new skill.

We introduce games played as individuals only after a group has had success in conversation and partner-game activities, and at a time when the group members are both comfortable with and interested in the point system. When we play these games, we make sure that the leaders are playing. It will be the leaders' role to demonstrate how to handle a lack of success in the game, and to comment (frequently – with smiles and laughter) about how much fun they are having even though luck is, unfortunately, going against them. Just as I did when my children were little and learning to play board games, I will often strategically make moves that are not very helpful in making me the winner. This insures that I will be able to comment frequently on how much fun I am having even though I am not winning.

---

2   These goals are explained in detail in Chapter 18.

Goals for individual games

- *Know when it is your turn* – Once again the ability to attend, stay focused, and be organized enough to follow the game so you know when it is your turn is crucial to success. Leaders need to be ready to prompt individuals about turns, and/or bring out the arrow and keep it pointed toward the player currently playing.

- *Ask for help* – The games often involve a strategy. Having an adult sit next to novice players to offer to help with decisions can lead to individuals learning to enjoy asking for advice and assistance.

- *Laugh a lot* – When I play games and luck turns against me, I will smile broadly while I "pretend" to be upset. Doing this in a broad or even slapstick manner initially engages some of the group members, and eventually all the participants begin to laugh at my antics. The next stage is for members to begin to imitate me. I then back off and let them become the focus of the fun.

An alternative goal (not often needed, but, when needed, essential) is:

- *Play fair and by the rules* – Some of our participants have been observed to cheat by moving game pieces or changing playing cards. Almost always, the leaders note this before the participants. My typical intervention is simply to watch, but then talk to the individual at the end of session or before the next session. I calmly explain what I observed, talk about how important it is to play fair, and let the participant know that I will add this additional goal the following week. I also let her know how proud we will both be next week when she works hard and sticks to the rules. This has been very effective. For the rare cases when it does not work, I tell the participant, "I guess we are trying to do something that is too hard for you right now. Next time we play this game, you and I will have fun doing an alternative activity. We'll try again together in a few weeks." This approach lets the child know that there is a problem, but doesn't shame or blame. I have never failed to help a child, over time, learn to play by the rules.

Rewards

We structure the group so that we will have two reward days per ten/eleven week session. Setting a goal of about 55 points usually works well. On the reward days we:

- Provide a treat that the group has helped select.

- Divide the rest of the time into two simultaneous activities. Half of the group plays a Wii game, and the other half selects a game they have enjoyed. We then switch so that everyone gets to play the Wii once.

Suggested activities

Conversation activities
- *Question Cards*
- *A Through Z Game*
- *Evaluation process*

Game activities
- *Up the River*
- *Pick It*
- *Mr. M's Minefield*
- *Bean Bag Toss*

Games played as individuals
- *Apples to Apples Junior*
- *Imaginiff*
- *Smart Ass*
- *Mr. M's Uno*
- *Moose in the House*
- *Kinder Bunnies*

Two-team games
- *Bean Bag Toss*
- *Bocce Ball* (weather permitting)

Chapter 22

Community-Based Groups for Junior High and Senior High Students

QUICK SNAPSHOT

Number of leaders	Three – at least one individual with a clinical degree or ASD certification. Two others who have been trained in Guiding Toward Growth principles. An older teen volunteer can be added as both a model and an additional resource. This is a good way to train older participants to become ready to be hired for group work.
Number of participants	Eight to twelve – I try to hold to eight if I have all junior high participants, about ten if I have a mixed group, and twelve if I have a group made up entirely of high school students.
Location	Large group room – including an area to sit in a circle, an area to sit around tables, and an open space to do some large group activities. Having a carpet on the floor is helpful (but not essential) in holding down the noise made by individuals and by chairs sliding across the floor.

Frequency	Once a week.
Length of sessions:	85–90 minutes.
Necessary materials	• Chairs
	• Metal white boards
	• Two or three square or rectangular tables (large enough for between four and six participants; able to be slid together for games requiring more participants and/or more table space to spread out materials)
	• Wii system
	• TV monitor for the Wii.
Duration of group	Groups are scheduled throughout the year in ten/eleven weekly sessions.[1]

These groups are the culmination of all the work that has gone before. Once a culture has been established by working with a core group in this format, or graduating participants from the younger community-based group, this group will be a time and place that teens will look forwards to attending. When it is working best, it will look a lot like a group of young people who have gotten together to have fun. Getting to that stage, however, requires work and planning.

Format

A goal for the adult leaders in this group is to get away from using the five-point rating scale as soon as possible. When I first began the community-based groups, I used the five-point rating scale for the first eleven-week session, and for half the second session. I then occasionally returned for refreshing purposes. I now have not used

---

1   I schedule my groups to coincide roughly with the seasons. I have a fall, winter, spring, and summer sessions.

the five-point scale in either the junior high or senior high group for three years.[2]

1. Gathering

We quickly discovered with community-based groups that we could not count on all the participants arriving on time. Some arrived early, some on time, some late, some quite late. It was frustrating trying to plan or use the time productively while we waited. We finally discovered using an initial puzzle or thinking mystery helped us to engage participants as they arrived. We wrote the thinking puzzle or riddle on the whiteboard, and challenged the participants to solve it as they arrived. This worked reasonably well, but now the difficulty was that some participants would work the problem, solve it, and then have nothing to do, and some would look at the problem, decide it was too hard, and pull out their iPods or hand-held video games.

A more successful intervention has been using *wuzzles* and *commonymns*.[3] Wuzzles are mixtures of words and drawings used to describe a familiar phrase. We would draw 5–6 wuzzles on a whiteboard and challenge participants to solve as many as they could.

Commonyms are groupings of three words, all of which have something in common. We presented a list of ten of these three-word pairings, and again challenged the participants to solve as many as they could.

These activities have been quite successful. Individuals who are quick to solve these were encouraged to solve as many as they could. It became apparent which individuals struggled with the logic and

---

2   Please review the material in Chapter 20, on "open-ended groups". Once we had successfully created a culture within the first group of cooperation, tolerance of differences, playing and partnering with anyone in the group, and setting differences by using compromising, we no longer needed to use the five-point system to reinforce it. The participants model the skills, and the leaders praise the use of the skills and coach participants toward success.

    I have discovered that this culture has successfully transferred to each new group I created. My sequence was:

    1. One junior high/senior high group.

    2. One junior high group; one senior high group (using the core of the first group to establish both groups.

    3. As the high school students aged and gained experience, I created the older high school/ transition age group that will be described in the next chapter.

    With the creation of each group, the core of "veteran" participants modeled skills to new participants, plus the willingness and enthusiasm to use those skills.

3   There are books with wuzzles, commonyms, lateral thinking puzzles, and riddles. I use www. wuzzlesandpuzzles.com to find the materials I need.

reasoning skills, and the adults could move to them and engage them individually in learning the reasoning skills required to solve one or two.

Regardless of what you choose, it will be important to have a "gathering" strategy.[4]

2. Planning

We make use of the whiteboard to plan the day's session. We usually begin with planning for using the Wii. During our groups, we will have three 20-minute sections on the Wii. Each participant can only play the Wii for one section. Since we have eight different Wii games, this discussion consists of limiting the choices, and then slotting participants into the sections. It is fun to watch the participants learn to make compromises, and also become willing to switch out of a favorite game in order to stay connected to a particular friend.

Once we have the Wii sections planned, we then are able to plan what we are going to do when we are not at the Wii. We encourage two or even three activities to be running concurrently. Leaders move individually to support the activities, or, by design and agreement, to support individuals. If we have four activities, the activity or game being played by our strongest individuals will be left without an adult. During those times we most likely will designate one person to act as the "leader". The leader's job is to come to one of the adults should any problem arise within the game.

Games and activities[5]

Wii games
- *Wii Sports*
- *WarioWare*
- *Mario Kart*

---

4   One strategy that did not work for us was "Starting on Time." We found that we organized and were ready to go, and then late arrivals came and forced us to re-think, and then re-think again. This was very frustrating to the participants, so we needed to come up with a productive and fun alternative.

5   See Part IV, *Materials and Activities*, for information about how these games are adapted to be used in *FunJoyment* groups.

- *Super Mario Brothers*
- *Raving Rabbids*
- *Boom Blox*
- *Boom Blox Bash Party*

Table games

- *Tsuro*
- *Pick It*
- *Moose in the House*
- *Mr. M's Uno*
- *Pit*
- *In a Pickle*
- *Perudo*
- *Killer Bunnies*
- *Dominion*
- *Playing-card games*
- *Fluxx card games*

Outdoor Games

- *Bocce Ball*
- *Frisbee Golf*

Whole-group games[6]

- *Apples to Apples*
- *Imaginiff*
- *Smart Ass*
- *Loaded Questions*
- *Sort it Out*
- *Twenty Questions*

---

6   The use of whole-group games will be described later in this chapter. For convenience, they are
    also listed here.

3. Switching to the next activity

Although the participants are practicing social interaction and social enjoyment skills constantly – and gaining competence and confidence in using these skills – in many ways I consider the skill of switching easily to the next activity to be the most important skill we are teaching. At the end of each 20-minute segment, whether the game is near being finished, and no matter at which "level" the players are at in the Wii game,[7] we switch.

Being able to shift to a new activity without completing the current activity is a skill that is generally very difficult for individuals with ASD, but it is a crucial work skill. I have had adults with ASD tell me that they have quit jobs because "the boss would never let me finish anything". Because switching to tasks is such a crucial work skill, we work on transitioning to different tasks something that we practiced multiple times each day.

4. Whole-group activities

The format described above involves our participants working in small groups. Due to the fact that future educational and employment opportunities usually require interacting occasionally in larger groups, we will make sure that we plan whole-group activities at least once every two or three weeks during one of the 20-minute segments. During these times, we schedule one of our activities that can include every participant. These include activities in which the participants play as individuals:

- *Apples to Apples*
- *Imaginiff*
- *Smart Ass*

or games in which we divide the large group into two teams to compete against each other:

---

7   We begin to announce switches about three minutes before each switch. The Wii game is usually the final determinant of the switch. The leader there keeps an eye on the clock, and makes a determination that the group is on its final race, world, game, or segment with about three minutes left in the section. She announces that to the Wii group, and then makes the announcement to the rest of the groups. The other leaders then begin reminding groups that only a few minutes remain, help determine winners, and solicit help packing up the games.

- *Loaded Questions*

- *Sort it Out*

- *Twenty Questions*

5. Qualities and compliments

As we near the end of a ten/eleven-week course of sessions, we begin a ritual of creating a small poster listing each participant's qualities and compliments. This replaces our gathering activity during the first 15 minutes of each group session. The format is for each individual to volunteer to be a person we focus on. We then ask each participant and each adult leader to make one statement of a quality about that person, or to give the person a compliment. We do three or four participants a week.

While the statements are being made, one leader writes them on the whiteboard. Writing on the whiteboard is crucial because our participants are stronger visual learners that auditory learners. They will learn much about making these statements, and add to their repertoire of "qualities and compliments", by reading what others have stated. They will also be better able to follow the process. This process allows them to know what has already been stated by referencing the whiteboard (instead of relying on their individual auditory memory).

While this is occurring, a second leader is writing the statements down so that small posters can be created for the participants to take home with them on the last day of the course.

This will be a difficult skill for the group members to learn and practice. There will be initial grumbling and dissatisfaction that will persist for many sessions. You will hear participants make statements such as:

> "This is stupid."
> "I don't want to hear anything about me."
> "I don't know anything about _____."
> "We know we all like each other."

I have learned to persist. Each time we begin and hear protests, I repeat my reasoning: this is a crucial work skill.

I truly believe this, for this reason: I have never had a job at which someone did not retire, resign, be promoted, be transferred, become engaged to be married, or experience a birth of a child. When this occurs there is often a celebration. Often at those celebrations, the custom is to begin to go around the table or around the room, and have each person state a quality or compliment about the individual who is the focus of the celebration. Individuals with ASD often experience "brain freeze" at these events. This can result in feeling embarrassed and anxious, and can lead those individuals to fear the next gathering.

I tell my group members that I want them to be prepared for those celebrations, ready to make their comment, and thus able to enjoy the celebration.

Expect that this will be a difficult skill for the group to learn, and be prepared for the adult to be ready with many possible suggestions. I train my staff to make suggestions to participants who are "stuck", and when the participant says, "Yeah, that one", to ask that individual to repeat the statement "using your own words". We will sometimes hear the same statement, and sometimes hear it repeated slightly differently. Regardless, we write the comment on the whiteboard and praise the member who made it.

I encourage you to stick with this expectation in these groups, because this is truly a work (and life) skill. Because the groups are open-ended, you will see improvement over time. You will also notice that new participants have an easier time learning this skill when they can watch the "veterans" come up with a comment with relative ease.

6. Extenders

Doing a community-based group creates the opportunity to create extensions of the group experience through involvement in the community. As described earlier, we offer volunteer coaching opportunities for teen participants through the Challenger Division of the local Little League, and Kelly Merges offers opportunities on Saturday for group members to play card games such as *Killer Bunnies* and *Dominion* at a local business. We have also supported the development of opportunities through the efforts of parents.

7. Parents

The parent component of the group has grown informally. Although many parents (particularly of our oldest participants) simply drop their youngsters off and pick them up later, many parents come from a distance and stay in the building during the groups. This has led to parents meeting informally and chatting during groups.

I decided to take advantage of this development by scheduling monthly half-hour parent groups that occur during the last 30 minutes of a designated group. My main objective is to have the parents meet each other, but there is always plenty to talk about. These meetings attract most of the parents – both those who stay and those who drop participants off. Together we have solved problems and given advice about home and school issues.

The parents have ended up extending the learning in the group in two principal ways. First, they have realized that the group is a ready pool of reliable peers to invite to birthday parties or just out for a Saturday pool or bowling party. Second, parents have become valuable resources to each other regarding summer camps, tutors, strategies, workshops and other helpful information. All of this has led to valuable opportunities for group participants to practice the skills they have developed in groups.

Chapter 23

Community-Based Groups for Older High Students and Young Adults

QUICK SNAPSHOT

Number of leaders	Two – at least one individual with a clinical degree or ASD certification, and one other who has been trained in *Guiding Toward Growth* principles. (The number of adult leaders is deliberately reduced in order to increase the independence of the groups members. The fact that many in this group will be trained volunteers to work in younger groups also helps this group function smoothly.)
Number of participants	Eight to twelve.
Location	Large group room – including an area to sit in a circle, an area to sit around tables, and an open space to do some large group activities. Having a carpet on the floor is helpful (but not essential) in holding down the noise made by individuals and by chairs sliding across the floor.

Frequency	Once a week.
Length of sessions	90 minutes.
Necessary materials	• Chairs
	• Metal whiteboards
	• Two or three square or rectangular tables (large enough for between four and six participants; able to be slid together for games requiring more participants and/or more table space to spread out materials.
	• Wii system
	• TV monitor for the Wii.
Duration of group	Groups are scheduled throughout the year in ten/eleven weekly sessions.[1]

This is the last group that I added to my community groups. I did not add this, or even imagine adding it, until my high school participants began to graduate from high school and join transition programs. At that time, they asked to be able to continue in a *FunJoyment* program.[2]

After consulting with their parents, I agreed to continue. But I also made a commitment to parents to deliberately add elements that were more "adult". I decided to make the group consist of 30 minutes of group talk/discussion, and 60 minutes of fun.

The first participants in this new group were "graduates" out of the high school group. It consisted of four older high school students and four high school graduates.

When we first met, they were not a happy bunch. They were disappointed to be leaving their treasured Depot Coffee House for a location that felt much more like a classroom.[3] During the first meetings, our discussion time consisted mainly of me trying to get

---

1   I schedule my groups to coincide roughly with the seasons. I have fall, winter, spring, and summer sessions.

2   In case you are curious, I am already thinking that I may need to add an "adult group" to graduate these young people into. Check my website in a few year to see the status of this.

3   I made the decision to move deliberately. I felt that learning new "adult" skills would be enhanced by leaving the "teen" location. Two years later, with the group having developed well and the participants happy with their new group, I believe it was a wise choice.

them to attend to a single topic (I used the whiteboard to chronicle our topic and discussion points as they arose) while they lapsed into side conversations and/or listened to their iPods. For topics, I asked them to offer possibilities. They offered few, and the ones suggested interested only a fraction of the group.

I did what I do well – I persisted and experimented.

I quickly made two determinations:

1.   The group was going to need to learn focus and discussion skills.

2.   Our topics had to be real and concrete. As much as their parents wanted them to discuss future events – attending college, moving into an apartment, getting a driver's license – I was not able to get them to become interested and focused unless the event was happening, or about to happen, to them.

I had limited success with my initial interventions. I then first taught – and we practiced – two strategies for group discussion:

- *The rule of fractions* – In short, any time there is a discussion going on, each individual should be talking for his fraction of the time. If there were eight participants, each person should be speaking for about one eighth of the time. If a participant is speaking more that one eighth of the time, he should consider restraining himself. If speaking less that one eighth of the time, the person should try to think of something to add.[4]

- *Comments and questions* – It was helpful to the group to learn that discussions move forwards based on comments and questions, and to learn the purpose of each. This seems to help when it is noted that someone has been relatively quiet for a while, and is prompted to join the discussion. Some have learned that they are most comfortable with comments, and some with questions.

With these skills taught, I then tried to get discussions going by role-playing. I told them to pretend I was a peer and had a problem. For example, my dad had lost his job, or my brother was using illegal drugs. We discovered that they were interested and asked good questions, but were totally thrown off and confused when I made up answers.

---

4   With the creation of this rule, the group quickly began to point out that I consistently break this rule by talking too much. I then tried to talk less, but together we discovered that I often need to rephrase and refocus the group. They still tease me good-naturedly about the fact that I "talk too much".

For example, they know I have brothers, but when I pretended my brother was chemically dependent, they got distracted about which brother had the problem. When I made it clear that I was pretending, many said that it was too confusing to talk about this because they know it was not true. The fact that I was pretending to be their age was very distracting for them. Eventually we stopped this strategy.

By accident, we discovered that we could talk about actual events that they were all aware of. A shooting on a college campus became a topic. So did the 2008 Presidential election. When a group member was looking for a job or taking a class at a community college, we could talk about it. I discovered we could work on the skills by talking about a current TV show, or a media star who had gone into chemical dependency treatment. Our discussion time picked up interest and momentum. Parents were disappointed that we were not preparing for apartment-living or college, but accepted that we most likely would not be able to talk about these things in the abstract. We had to wait until someone was applying to college, looking for work, or had an issue in their own family.

Today, our discussion time is often (but not always) about minor topics. But the participants are engaged, and smile and laugh during the 30 minutes of "talk time". Although most prefer the game time, there have been few complaints about our "talk time". I have discovered that one real life experience I can use frequently is the introduction of a new member to the group. The first time I added a member to this group, I discovered that even though participants had been together for years and enjoyed each other's company, they had retained little knowledge about their peers' lives. I decided to use the introduction of new group members as a time to practice the skill of introducing a group member to the new participant. Group members select one another, and tell the new person:

- the name of their peer
- what town or city she lives in
- something about her family
- where she goes to school or work
- a group activity she enjoys
- something they like or admire about the person they are introducing.

Discussion skills are improving each week, as are the complementary listening skills. The group is slowly finding its way.

One clear piece of evidence of the growth in these skills is the ease with which this group moves through the process of identifying qualities and compliments[5] for each other. What occurs very slowly in the teen groups – taking three weeks and using at least 15 minutes of group time each week – has been accomplished at one meeting in less than a half-hour in this group. The skills the participants display in staying focused, thinking ahead, and having something genuine and thoughtful to say is remarkable.

After discussion time, we have fun time. This works nearly the same as the enjoyment time with the high school group, with these important differences:

1. Within the 60 minutes of fun time we have two 30-minute sections. Because there is much to choose from, there is more need for compromising and negotiating.

2. The leaders deliberately back off in the planning. Group members are expected to negotiate and begin by themselves. These young people set up the Wii, put the game discs into the console, and negotiate themselves which variations to use. We keep all the other games in bins. The participants who are not playing the Wii unpack the materials and discuss/ negotiate which ones to use.

3. Participants are encouraged to bring in favorite games and teach us how to play.

4. When the session is over, participants are expected to pack up the games, pack up the Wii, and help us get everything out to my car.

Just as in the high school group, we will sometimes schedule an "all play" game so that all group members interact with each other. I schedule these activities during the discussion time, because they are often based on laughing and talking together. Interestingly, this group expresses more enjoyment of the "all group" activity than the younger group. Perhaps this is a sign of developing maturity.

See the previous chapter for a list of the recommended games and activities.

---

5   See Chapter 17 for the complete description of the qualities and compliments ritual.

Part IV

Materials and Activities

Chapter 24

Sample Permission Letters

When doing school groups, parent permission is usually required to involve neurotypical students in the groups. Over the years I have used these letters in order to obtain permission.

The sample letters vary in levels of accountability. Working with teachers, I have discovered that if there are any complaints, they will come to the classroom teacher. Therefore, I always ask the classroom teacher to decide which letter will be used. In some cases, the school administrator may want to make the decision regarding the letter selection.

General Permission Letter

School name
Street address
City, State, Zip
Telephone: 000 000 0000

Date

Dear families of (*teacher's name*) students,

We are beginning a small group experience for some of the students in your child's class. The group will meet for a half-hour weekly and will focus on developing friendship and social interaction skills. Some students were selected because their parents have identified specific social goals. These students will be permanent members of our group. Other students will rotate through the group and stay for about six sessions (roughly six weeks). Some students will be selected because (*teacher's name*) feels they will benefit from learning and practicing social interaction skills, and other students will be selected because they model good peer interaction skills.

Children generally enjoy the activities and attention they receive while they are part of this group. It is a time that concentrates on learning social interaction skills that will help them be more successful in school and in life.

The group has been scheduled at a time that will not interfere with students' academic progress.

If you have any questions or concerns about this group, or if you would like to suggest that your child join this group, please call one of us.

Sincerely,

Name   Name
Social Worker/Special Ed. Teacher   Classroom Teacher
Telephone number   Telephone number

Permission Letter Seeking Only a Negative Reply

School name
Street address
City, State, Zip
Telephone: 000 000 0000

Date

Dear families of (*teacher's name*) students,

We are beginning a small group experience for some of the students in your child's class. The group will meet for a half-hour weekly and will focus on developing friendship and social interaction skills. Some students were selected because their parents have identified specific social goals. These students will be permanent members of our group. Other students will rotate through the group and stay for about six sessions (roughly six weeks). Some students will be selected because (*teacher's name*) feels they will benefit from learning and practicing social interaction skills, and other students will be selected because they model good peer interaction skills.

Children generally enjoy the activities and attention they receive while they are part of this group. It is a time that concentrates on learning social interaction skills that will help them be more successful in school and in life.

The group has been scheduled at a time that will not interfere with students' academic progress.

During the course of the year we hope to include as many children as possible. Please fill out the slip below if you *do not* want your child to participate in this experience this year.

If you have any questions or concerns about this group, or if you would like to suggest that your child join this group, please call one of us.

Sincerely,

Name   Name
Social Worker/Special Ed. Teacher   Classroom Teacher
Telephone number   Telephone number

- -

Dear (*teacher's name*)
Please do not schedule my child, _____, in
friendship/social interaction group this year.

_____
(Parent signature)

Permission Letter Seeking Only a Positive Reply

School name
Street address
City, State, Zip
Telephone: 000 000 0000

Date

Dear families of (*teacher's name*) students,

We are beginning a small group experience for some of the students in your child's class. The group will meet for a half-hour weekly and will focus on developing friendship and social interaction skills. Some students were selected because their parents have identified specific social goals. These students will be permanent members of our group. Other students will rotate through the group and stay for about six sessions (roughly six weeks). Some students will be selected because (*teacher's name*) feels they will benefit from learning and practicing social interaction skills, and other students will be selected because they model good peer interaction skills.

Children generally enjoy the activities and attention they receive while they are part of this group. It is a time that concentrates on learning social interaction skills that will help them be more successful in school and in life.

The group has been scheduled at a time that will not interfere with students' academic progress.

During the course of the year we hope to include as many children as possible. Please fill out the slip below to give us permission to include your child at some time this year.

If you have any questions or concerns about this group, or if you would like to suggest that your child join this group, please call one of us.

Sincerely,

Name   Name
Social Worker/Special Ed. Teacher   Classroom Teacher
Telephone number   Telephone number

- -

Dear (*teacher's name*)
You have my permission to include my child, _____, in friendship/social interaction group at some point this year.

_____
(Parent signature)

Permission as a Group is Starting

School name
Street address
City, State, Zip
Telephone: 000 000 0000

Date

Dear families of (*teacher's name*) students,

We are beginning a small group experience for some of the students in your child's class. The group will meet for a half-hour weekly and will focus on developing friendship and social interaction skills. Some students were selected because their parents have identified specific social goals. These students will be permanent members of our group. Other students will rotate through the group and stay for about six sessions (roughly six weeks). Some students will be selected because (*teacher's name*) feels they will benefit from learning and practicing social interaction skills, and other students will be selected because they model good peer interaction skills.

Children generally enjoy the activities and attention they receive while they are part of this group. It is a time that concentrates on learning social interaction skills that will help them be more successful in school and in life.

The group has been scheduled at a time that will not interfere with students' academic progress.

We would like to invite your child to be a part of our group for the next six weeks. Please sign below to give your permission for that to occur.

If you have any questions or concerns about this group, please call one of us.

Sincerely,

Name   Name
Social Worker/Special Ed. Teacher   Classroom Teacher
Telephone number   Telephone number

- -

Dear (*teacher's name*)
I give my permission for my child, _____, to be part of Friendship/Social Interaction Group for the next six weeks.

_____   _____
(date)   (Parent signature)

Chapter 25

Scoreboard

Directions

1. Draw scoreboard graphic on card stock.

2. Before laminating, use a red sharpie or marker to color the universal "no" symbol over the "squiggly line" graphic.

3. Laminate.

4. Cut the graphic in half along the vertical midline.

5. Tape top and bottom portions together.

6. Attach magnetic tape or magnets to the completed card.

7. Create magnetic plastic jewels (80 are recommended to start) to be used to reinforce the behaviors at group.

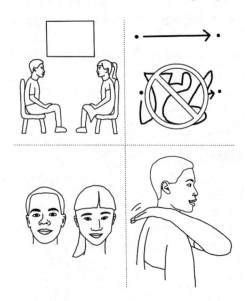

Chapter 26

Activities for Five-, Six- and Seven-Year-Olds

Suggested order in which to do the activities:

> *Big Dice*
>
> *Ask to Play*
>
> *Charades*
>
> *Ask for Help*
>
> *Ask to Share*
>
> *Interrupting an Adult*
>
> *Bean Bag Toss*

BIG DICE

Big Dice is a wonderful game to be played as the first activity every time a new group is formed. The visual memory required is often a strength for students with ASD, and, since they are ongoing group members, their skills increase each time they play. This is a game in which the students with ASD can eventually help the neurotypical students new to group and who are playing for the first time.

Required materials

- A big dice – I make mine by squaring off the top of a half-gallon milk or juice container, and covering the surface with contact paper.

- Between 12 and 15 pictures of animals and/or objects (4" x 6"). Ask speech/language therapists for some, or buy them at a learning supply store.

- Four pieces of construction paper (5" x 7") – four different colors. (Laminate these for durability.)

- Four strips of the same colors above to tape to the four long sides of the big dice you have constructed. (Cover the whole carton with clear shipping tape – again for durability.)

- Magnetic tape or dots.

Place enough tape or magnetic dots on each picture to insure it will stick to the whiteboard.

Place the tape or dots around the outer edge of the construction paper. (These need to fit over the pictures and stick firmly to the whiteboard.)

Object of the game

Four pictures will always be covered by the four pieces of construction paper. Players take turns tossing the big dice to the floor in front of them. They must then try to remember what is under the color that ends face up on the dice. If they successfully remember, they move the construction paper to a different picture.

Play

1. Select the number of pictures you think appropriate for your group. Generally, younger students do better with between six and eight pictures; older student can do 12 or even more. (Warning: even at 12, the adult leaders will have trouble remembering.)

2. Display the pictures on the whiteboard. Leave enough space between the pictures for the construction paper pieces to be placed over them. Make sure everyone knows what the pictures depict. (One way to do this is to go around the group sequentially displaying the pictures to the students, and asking for the identification before you display them on the whiteboards.)

3. Beginning with an adult, take a piece of construction paper and cover one picture. While doing so, state, "This is a memory game, not a guessing game. We have to know what is hidden and try to remember. So I will show you what I am covering, and tell you what I am covering – because some people remember what they see, and some people remember what they hear."

4. The adult then gives another piece of construction paper to the child next to her, and asks the child to do the same – emphasizing that all need to see and hear.

5. This process continues sequentially to the next two children in the group. Finally four pictures are covered.

6. The next child becomes the first "contestant". This child tosses the big dice and has to try to remember the picture under the color that ends up on top.

    • *Straight line* behavior for this game is thinking while sitting, and announcing your answer before you get up

    • If a child does not remember, she can ask for hints. People wanting to give hints raise their hands. The player gets to pick on someone to give a hint. A player can ask for as many hints as necessary. *Important*: giving a hint is a *straight line* behavior, and is immediately rewarded with a jewel on the scoreboard.[1]

7. If the player uncovers the picture and is correct, she moves the construction paper to another picture. If the person is wrong, the construction paper goes back on the same picture.

8. Play continues until all the students have had an equal number of turns.

9. Applause and clapping are encouraged.

---

1   Young children often have to learn what a hint is. I keep repeating that a hint is a description or characteristic of the picture. An animal sound is a hint. Telling us the letter sound the animal or object begins with is a hint. Clever hints should be celebrated with praise and applause.

Tips

- Some students may not be able to keep from uttering the animal/object under the construction paper once they think about it. These students need extra individual practice, and sometimes need to learn to hold their lips shut with their fingers as they develop this skill. The adults need to be sensitive to this, and make sure it is not viewed as acting out or cheating.

- Adults should occasionally pretend not to remember when it is their turn so they can model asking for help.

- Adults should raise their hands when students are stuck in order to model giving effective hints. (With their strong memory skills, some students with ASD will remember a hint for months or years, and will use it appropriately on another day, impressing their classmates.)

- Sometimes (not often) the big dice lands on end – with no color displayed. This is a time for great excitement – the adult announces that because of that lucky toss, that person gets to decide which of the four colors to play.

ASK TO PLAY (ROLE-PLAY)

Ask to Play is an excellent first role-play to do with a new group, or a group that is continuing with students with identified needs but with new neurotypical students. It works well to play *Big Dice* at the first session, and do *Ask to Play* at the second.

Asking a peer to play is an important connection skill, and a skill that can be easily transferred to the playground or the classroom. Students with ASD often lack the skills in:

- planning

- specific speech/language phrasing

- knowing how to start and (perhaps more importantly) stop

- enjoying cooperative play.

This lesson is designed to both teach the skills, and reinforce the fun.

Materials needed

- Three play objects – for example, a foam ball, a foam frisbee (simply made by cutting a frisbee-sized disc out of one-inch foam bought at a fabric store), and a soft plastic truck or car.

- The poster (see example on page 168) outlining the three steps in the role-play:

    1. Pick out a toy, and take it with you.

    2. Walk up to the person you want to play with.

    3. Ask, "Will you play with me?"

Group process

1. The leaders begin session with the *Ready to start* and *Compliments* ritual using the scoreboard. The leaders then let the students know that everyone will all be practicing the important skill of asking someone to play with them. Emphasis should be given to the fact that this is fun, and that everyone will get a chance.

2. The leaders then demonstrate how to play with the objects. Move behind or to the side of the semicircle of chairs at this point – simply to give the students a bit more room. Demonstrate that:

    - The ball can be rolled or tossed,

    - The frisbee is tossed with a flick of the wrist, and

    - The truck is always rolled.

3. They also demonstrate rolling or tossing to each other for four turns, and they count the turns aloud.

4. The three objects are then placed on a small table, desk, chair, or stool by the side of the semicircle of participants.

5. The leaders then point to the three steps on the poster, and explain that *straight line* jewels will be given for each step. Jewels are placed on the whiteboard right beside each step

after each role-play. Doing so creates a visual reminder of each step after each role-play.

6. The leaders do the role-play first. Having predetermined who will be the person who asks, that person walks to the objects, and selects one. That person then walks up to the other adult, displays the object, and says, "Will you play (*ball, frisbee, truck*) with me?"

7. The second leader expresses delight at being asked, and the pair walk to the designated play spot. There they take four turns. The adults then smile, say "Thanks" and "You're welcome", and perhaps add to the fun by slapping hands or fist bumping. They then return the object to the table and sit down.

8. One leader asks the group if they saw each step – and when a student identifies the steps, the leader places a jewel to the right of that step on the poster. (Bonus space can be created under the poster to reinforce the "Thank you"/"You're welcome" and/or the hand slap as well as the steps.)

9. The leader who was asked to play, now becomes the "asker". That leader repeats step six, but asks the student perceived to have the strongest behavioral and social skills to play. When finished, this pair returns to the circle, and jewels are placed alongside the poster steps.

10. Following this, the student who was asked to play becomes the "asker". The student is told that the adults have had a turn, so pick someone who has not yet played.

11. The process continues, with the student who was asked to play always becoming the "asker", until all have had a turn.

12. The leaders then move into the *Praising yourself* and *Counting the jewels* process.

Tips

- One student will be the last chosen, and thus the last to be the "asker". Turn this into an advantage by announcing, "Wow, _____ has been very patient and is now last. The reward for being last is that, since everyone has now had a turn, _____ gets to ask anyone in the group to play!"

- Once the group has progressed to the students playing, one adult should stay in the play area in case a child needs support in tossing or rolling, or in case a child needs support in stopping and returning the object.

- Sometimes (especially if this is the first time that a student with ASD has participated in this role-play) a student will refuse to take a turn. That student should be encouraged, but not forced. The leader should then give that student *straight line* jewels for watching.

- If you know that a particular combination might not work well, be directive as to who is to be selected in order to avoid that match-up.

- Do everything you can to maximize the fun – laugh at errant frisbee throws, get the whole group to count turns aloud, applaud catches, etc.

Ask to Play – Poster

CHARADES

Charades is an activity that promotes using and observing body language. I like to use the cards from the game *Kids on Stage* (available commercially) for this activity.

There are three groups of cards in this game. Young children do best if you limit their choices to animals or actions and eliminate the cards pertaining to objects.

Explain to the students that all will get to be the actors in turn. Persons who guess correctly will not get the next turn.

Straight line behavior (the behaviors that will be rewarded with jewels) in this activity are:

- waiting/watching while sitting
- raising hands to indicate you want to guess
- waiting to be called upon to make a guess.

In order to help the students when it is their turn to pantomime, one leader should:

1. Sit in front of the whiteboard with the two stacks of cards.

2. Invite the players to come up, turn and face the group, and then look at the card (otherwise some in the audience often get a look at the card).

3. Let the players know that it is okay to make animal noises when acting out an animal (since many animals have four legs or two legs and two wings).

4. Make suggestions/offer to pantomime with the player if the guessers are stuck.

5. If the actor is having a lot of difficulty, demonstrate actions and ask the student to follow along.

Important: students will do better and better as this activity is repeated. This will lead to increasing opportunities to compliment others and make expressions of self-praise.

ASK FOR HELP (ROLE-PLAY)

Ease and confidence asking for help is an important social interaction skill. This role-play focuses on this skill by reinforcing these three steps:

1. Approach and look directly at the person you would like to help you.

2. State the problem. Ask for help.

3. Say "Thank you" and "You're welcome".

This skill can be practiced with many scenarios. These include:

- A student has brought a favorite stuffed animal to school for sharing. Now it is time to get on the buses to go home, and the student discovers he failed to put the animal in his backpack. Help is needed to find it quickly. (Letting students take turns being the teacher in this scenario adds to the fun.)

- A child goes to a candy store with a friend. There they "buy" cardboard cutouts of candy. When they go to pay, one student discovers that she has left her money at home. She asks her friend for help lending her the money – she will then go right home and retrieve her money. (Having a cash register and letting students take turns being the shopkeeper adds to the fun.)

- A teacher notices that blocks/beanbags have been left in a play area, and asks a child to clean up the mess. The child tosses all the objects into a bin, and then discovers that the bin is "too heavy" to be lifted by one person. (The leader here introduces that this is real acting – just like in the movies. The bin is obviously not too heavy, but with real acting we will convince the audience that it is too heavy.) The student asks a second student for help, and together they wrestle the heavy bin to its resting place on a table. (Again, rotating the role of teacher adds to the fun.)

Ask for Help – Poster

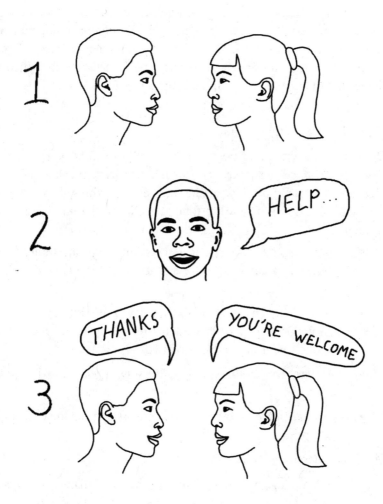

ASK TO SHARE (ROLE-PLAY)

Asking to share in an activity is an important social skill. Many of our students come to us with skills in being able to accept sharing something, but with limited skill or practice in problem-solving a situation by suggesting a way to share. This role-play provides that practice.

As the poster illustrates, there are two basic ways in which a suggestion of how to share can be made:

- splitting something in half

- doing an activity in turn.

Discuss the activities and point out how silly it would be to use the "wrong" way to suggest sharing – it would be silly to break a sled into pieces, and it would be silly to take turns eating a candy bar.

Practice this role-play using four possibilities[2] that motivate most children:

- *Graham crackers* – Pretend it is snack time and one student has brought a graham cracker for a snack, and another student has forgotten a snack.

- *Chalk* – The chalk is used to draw a picture on colored construction paper. Both students have a piece of paper, but only one student has a piece of chalk.

- *A marble ramp* – In this role-play there is a great ramp, but only one marble.

- *A plastic periscope* – Obviously only one person can look through the scope at a time.

The poster describes three steps:

1. Walk up to the person and ask to play/share the object. (The person responds with, "I'm sorry, but there is only one _____.")

2. The student then has to think of which of the two solutions to suggest.[3]

3. Make your suggestion.

---

2   I use only two at a time – one that can be split, and one that requires turn-taking.

3   It is a good idea to teach the students a "thinking posture". Step 2 in the poster depicts one "thinking posture", but there are obviously others. This is a way both to cue people that you are thinking and also to recognize the body language of someone who is signaling that she is thinking.

Ask to Share – Poster

INTERRUPTING AN ADULT (ROLE-PLAY)

Students with ASD are often very aggressive when they want to get the attention of an adult. Many adults reinforce this either by allowing interruptions or by negatively reinforcing an interruption – which is likely to be misinterpreted by the child.

This lesson teaches the basic skill of learning to wait by giving the student a clear direction and expectation – in other words, giving the student a positive direction and an understandable experience.

This role-play is set up for an adult to be busy – in this case by reading a book or report. Since the students will all get to play the part of the teacher, it is important to pick a book or document with which they have some understanding and/or comfort.

Also needed are:

- two different colored chairs

- a question to be answered – such as:

  o When is the field trip?

  o When will we be celebrating my birthday?

The role-play proceeds in this fashion:

1. The person playing the teacher is sitting reading the book or report.

2. The person playing the student approaches, and waits quietly.

3. When the "teacher" doesn't respond, the "student" says, "Excuse me."

4. The "teacher" responds, but states, "I'm sorry. I have to focus on this report. Could you please go sit in the _____ colored chair. I will let you know when I'm ready."

5. The "student" goes and sits for 15–20 seconds.

6. The teacher then calls the student over, and the student asks the prepared question.

The poster elements are:

- Walk close and stand quietly.

- Say "Excuse me."

- Listen to the teacher's instructions.

Interrupting an Adult (poster)

BEAN BAG TOSS

Bean Bag Toss is an activity that is exciting and enjoyable for students from kindergarten through high school. The difficulty of the game can be regulated by the distance placed between the throwers and the targets.

The best location for the game is the floor directly beneath a whiteboard. (The white board should have a chalk ledge.)

The targets could be:

- A plastic crate that is placed against the wall as the primary target. Landing in this is worth one point.

- A bin approximately the same perimeter as the crate, but not as tall, is the target worth three points. This is placed in front of the one-point crate.

- Two long but narrow bins (the narrow width facing the throwers) placed on each side of the one-point crate. These targets are worth five points.

- Any bean bag that lands on the chalk ledge is worth ten points. (Hint: remove these bean bags once they have landed – they cannot be knocked off, and their removal makes it easier to land additional bean bags on the ledge.)

Play

The group is divided into two teams. Each team will send up one thrower at a time. Teams are established, and each team is helped in creating a throwing order. While two opponents are throwing, everyone else must be sitting. Each team has three or four bean bags.

Once the two opponents come to the throwing area, they:

1. Decide together the distance from which they will throw. (Use a chalk or whiteboard eraser to mark that spot.)

2. Decide who will throw first.

3. Alternate throwing their bean bags.

The adult announces the running score after each throw. When the contest is over, the adult writes the score on the whiteboard, and the two throwers retrieve the bean bags and give them to the next two contestants. (*Note:* this small point is a big safety factor. If more than two students rush to the bins and bend over, it is easy for someone to lose their balance and fall into the chalk ledge – and that hurts!)

As students play, reinforce good sportspersonship:

- We will cheer for/encourage everyone.

- We will never boo or shout out when someone is throwing.

- We always give each other a high five and say something like "Good game".

Chapter 27

Activities for All Other Groups

The activities for all the remaining groups are listed here. Because there is some overlap in activities between age groups, activities are listed in alphabetical order. Please see the listing at the end of the chapters describing each group for the activities recommended for each age group.

A THROUGH Z GAME

A through Z is a deceptively easy game that many students very much enjoy. Playing the game reinforces some skills that are very difficult to teach:

- staying focused on the group task even when it is not your turn
- planning ahead so that the group can complete the task as quickly as possible.

These are very important school and social interaction skills. The fact that students are practicing them while having a lot of fun makes this game a very valuable resource.

The game is played with the group arranged around a whiteboard, chalkboard, or large sheet of paper.

On the board or paper, the leader writes out the alphabet three or four times. An order of answering is established (adults included) and the game is explained. The group chooses a category, and then attempts to erase or cross out the alphabet by coming up with one item in the category that starts with every letter in the alphabet. *Important:*

as the game progresses, the game gets more difficult because players have increasingly fewer possible choices, and the letters that end up remaining at the end are often very difficult.

The adults should model thinking ahead:

- Always use a few minutes before starting an alphabet to think of choices.

- Underline letters that will be difficult.

The adult should also model encouraging all the players, and celebrating when a clever or difficult letter is erased.

Suggested categories are listed below. The first are the easiest, and the last is the hardest:

- boys' names

- girls' names

- animals

- foods

- places

- character names.

APPLES TO APPLES

Apples to Apples can be purchased commercially. For my youngest groups, and with groups that include older participants with cognitive delays, I use *Apples to Apples Junior*. I play the variation of the game that has the players sharing the opportunity to be the "judge" in an established (clockwise or counterclockwise) fashion, rather than have the "winner" of a round become the judge. I do this in order to emphasize that the fun of the game is being the judge and laughing a lot rather than collecting green cards.

These are the whiteboard goals:

- Think about the judge. (Is this person a literal person? A sarcastic person? An "off the wall" person?)

- Listen – when the judge reads the category card, and when the judge reads all the response cards.

- Have fun and laugh a lot.

Leaders should model and practice how to listen to each response card as it is read, and model how to comment as the response cards are read, and then comment on what they are learning about the person as he judges.

BEAN BAG TOSS

This is the same game explained earlier in this book as part of the youngest participants' groups (page 176). It is included here because the young people enjoy it so much and frequently ask to play this game as older elementary students, junior high students, and even high school students. The senior and junior high students often get very inventive about choosing the spot from which they will be shooting – quite a distance away, or throwing at the targets from an angle. All of this adds to the fun.

Suggested goals for this activity are:

- Be "okay" with your teammates.

- Cheer for/encourage everyone – not just your teammates.

- Have fun whether you win the round or not.

BOCCE BALL

Bocce Ball has been an invaluable addition to our *FunJoyment* activities. Many of our young people struggle with large and/or small motor skills, and some who possess good skills have difficulty with the subtle rules and strategies of team sports. Bocce Ball is a slow-paced, strategic lawn game that almost all of our group members have learned to enjoy. In order to accommodate different skill and strength levels, I have invested in three different Bocce Ball sets:

- a light beginner set with smaller, plastic balls

- a recreational set with light, traditional-sized balls

- A "professional" set – official size and weight.

In addition to learning to enjoy playing, this game teaches players how to cooperate in order to determine which team is closest to the ball in order to determine first which team should throw, and then which team has scored points (and how many). It is a good idea to include a rope or tape measure in your Bocce Ball set, and, during play, invite members of each team to help determine which team in closest to the target ball. The goal is for the older participants eventually to play the game without a group leader being the "referee", but simply to be out enjoying the game.

In addition to learning to enjoy this game at our groups, a number of families have purchased Bocce sets for use in the backyards and parks near their homes, and also to use when friends and relatives visit.

Suggested goals for Bocce Ball in school-based groups or with the youngest community-based groups are:

- Be "okay" with your teammate(s).

- Cheer for/encourage everyone.

- Have fun, no matter what the result.

DOMINION

Dominion is a commercially available card game that teaches strategic thinking and complex planning. The basic game can be played with four players, but by adding expansion packs, the complexity and the number of players can be increased. This game cannot be played within a 30-minute time period, so I never play this game in a school-based group. I introduce this game for high school and older participants, and schedule it for two of the 20-minute play sessions.

I play this game with no adaptations with the exception that the game is ended by time expiring rather than by finishing through card depletion.

FIRST/LAST GAME

This is a game I often use when students are eating a treat that they have earned, or we are celebrating a birthday or holiday. This game can be played while the students are grouped around a table. If they are at a table, make sure the students with ASD are seated so that they are facing the whiteboard.

The idea of this game is to make the longest possible "chain" of items in a category, naming each progressive item by using the last letter of the item that precedes it. For example, if the category is animals, *cat* could lead to *tiger,* which could lead to *rooster,* which could lead to *rat.* The leader keeps track of the letters on the whiteboard. In the above example the letters posted would be: C T R R T.

Making a rule that a word cannot be used twice helps prevent "loops". It is also helpful to allow a person who is "stuck" to change categories so that play can go on. Most students get very excited when there is a chain of 25–30 letters on the board.

Hint: I have discovered that when the category is *places,* long chains of the letter "A" can be made, since so many places start and end with A (Alaska, Alabama, Asia, Africa, Australia, Aurora, Antarctica, Austria, etc.). It is a lot of fun when the students make this discovery.

FRISBEE GOLF

Frisbee Golf can be a lot of fun to play if you have participants who can throw a Frisbee, and if the weather is not too windy. I use better grade Frisbees (free and less expensive Frisbees can be too light and unevenly balanced, so buying good Frisbees is generally a good idea). For the target, I use an orange traffic cone.

I place the cone for the first "hole", and, from that point on, the low "golfer" is rewarded by being allowed to place the cone for the next hole. Players can get quite creative in placing the cone – on top of slides, under swings, and behind fences. Have fun.

Suggested goals for a school-based group or a younger community-based group are:

- Wait to throw (remember the person who is farthest from the hole plays – just like in golf).

- Try your best – laugh when your shot goes awry.

- Have fun, no matter what your score is.

IMAGINIFF

Imaginiff is a commercially available game that I play almost as described in the printed directions. The only change I make is to eliminate the Bonus cards and the Challenge section on the game board (I simply write in a name over the word "Challenge").

Rotate the reading of the cards consecutively around the group so that everyone gets a chance to be the "leader". If someone has difficulty reading, place an adult right next to that player in order to provide support. Go through the cards and screen out questions based on trivia that only adults might know, and also for answers that are lengthy and thus potentially more difficult to understand and remember.

When the youngest groups begin to play *Imaginiff* support them by writing the six possible selections on the whiteboard. As their skills in listening and holding the selections in their mind increase, move to passing the card around the table so that multiple players can look at it simultaneously.

This is a terrific game for working on listening skills and remembering verbal information. It also promotes thinking about how others view the situation – thus it is a way to help the players learn beginning empathy skills.

Sometimes beginning players will focus on doing well and "winning" the first few times the game is played, but all eventually learn that the fun of the game is the laughter at the ridiculous answers.

When playing at a school or with young beginning players, use these three goals:

- Listen while the question and selections are read.

- Think about how everyone in the room might answer.

- Have fun, no matter the result.

IN A PICKLE

In a Pickle is also available commercially. I do not use this in any school-based group. This is a word card game that promotes flexible thinking, and we use it in order to try to get as outrageous as possible. This game is great to use in community groups when there is a small group of players who want to do something different than playing the Wii or playing a large-group game. It is useful for building relationship with a newer member of a group.

INTRODUCTORY QUESTIONS

These are questions I use at the first meeting of school groups – late elementary, junior high and senior high. This serves four purposes. First, it is a ritual that students with ASD come to rely on to get past the initial anxiety of meeting three or four new peers. Second, it allows students with ASD to practice using the question/answer ritual to meet new people. Third, it allows participants to work on different and/or more sophisticated answers to the questions. Finally, it allows me to observe the students who are new to me, and to make some beginning decisions about how I will seat and team individuals at future meetings.

Seat the students in a semicircle around a whiteboard, and write these goals on the board:

- Wait for your turn.

- Listen with your ears and your eyes. (Encourage all listeners to look at the person speaking, and also point out that speakers should be rotating their gaze to all listeners. Many students are conditioned to look at adults when answering in school, and those will be prompted by a gesture to look around at the other students while they are speaking.)

- Be brief – short answers will mean more turns.

Each question is answered by every group member. Every student gets to give the answer first once, and that person decides whether to move around the group clockwise or counterclockwise. Use these questions:

- "Tell us who is in your family – the family that is at your home or apartment when you go home. Some of you might have two families if your parents are separated or divorced. Remember to tell us about pets – they are very important family members."

- "If you had a magic wand and could turn yourself into an animal for a day, what animal would you choose? Why?"

- "If you were going to take us all out to dinner, where would you take us and what would you suggest we eat?"

- "If you had a magic wand and could select to have one (and only one) magical or superpower, which power would you choose?"

- "If you had the power to change precipitation from clouds from rain or snow to anything you want, what would you choose to fall instead of rain or snow?"

- "If you could have one great talent – be the best in the world at a sport, music, dance, acting, etc. – what talent would you want?"

- If you won a contest and were able to take all of us on an all-expense-paid vacation to a location anywhere in the world, where would you take us?

KILLER BUNNIES

Killer Bunnies is a complex commercially available game. It includes a starter pack and many expansion packs.

I must admit, I do not understand and cannot play this game. The younger staff members I have hired have taught this game to many of the individuals in my teenage and young adult community-based groups. It is a long game – when players decide to play this game, they sign up for two of our 20-minute sessions.

I was reluctant to bring this game into groups because I did not understand how to play it, and therefore it is something I felt I would not be able to control well. My younger staff members convinced me to include this game. I am glad they did.

For many of our group members, the fact that the details on the hundreds of playing cards needs to be remembered plays into their strong detail memory skills. It turns out that about a third of our participants love this game.

An additional strength of this game is that we have used the playing of this game to link members to game players in the community who play it on weekends.

KINDER BUNNIES

Kinder Bunnies is a beginner game that helps the 11- and 12-year-olds get ready to learn the much more complex *Killer Bunnies*. This game is not as difficult – I understand it and can play it. This game generally takes a bit more than 20 minutes, so when it is played, plan for a more flexible schedule. Suggested goals are:

- Know when it is your turn.

- Be fair – do not pick on one person with the attack cards.

- Laugh when something goes wrong.

LOADED QUESTIONS

This is a commercially available game. However, I never play it as it is designed. I bought it just to get access to the questions in the game. I have used this activity in both school-based and community-based groups.

Use the questions in the following manner:

- Divide the group into two equal groups. Assign an adult leader to each group. (If it is necessary to equalize the groups, assign one adult to play in one group, and the other to coordinate only in the other.)

- A question is read, and then the groups are set to work. The direction is that each group member must answer the question, and the answers must be written down and numbered.

- The answers to the questions are read aloud, and the leader writes the numbered answers on the whiteboard.

- The groups then reconvene with the task of guessing which member of the opposing team gave which of the listed answers.

- Once the groups have made their determinations, the answers are read and the team with the most correct answers is declared the winner.

This is not an easy activity. Group members will have great difficulty attending both to the discussion needed to create the answers, and then to the discussion needed to decide about the answers. This is why this activity is valuable. Neither task comes easily to individuals with ASD, so practicing and getting better at these skills will be helpful in developing the discussion and verbal memory skills that will be helpful in future work environments.

When using this activity in schools and with younger participants, suggested goals are

- Listen to each other.

- Think about what you know about the members of the other group.

- Make decisions together.

MR. M'S MINEFIELD

Minefield is a great activity for reinforcing:

- working together in a group

- paying attention when it is not your turn

- discovering the right answer by making mistakes – which eventually then lead you to the correct answer.

Minefield is an activity I have seen used at youth camps and as a team-building activity used for businesses and organizations. In those instances, a grid is developed on a tarp using duct-tape. I use a *Twister*[1] mat as the minefield. I have discovered that using the *Twister* mat, with the spots in four colors, assists my participants in both remembering the path, and in being able to communicate the path to their teammates.

Use one whiteboard or one portion of a large whiteboard to identify the task and directions:

- Everyone must get through the minefield.

- Turns must be taken, so an order has to be established and then be maintained.

---

1   *Twister* is a commercially available game. It is readily available at toy stores, but I have discovered it many times at garage and rummage sales.

- Everyone will need help – there is too much for any one person to remember.

- Once on the board, the next step will have to be to an adjacent spot (see diagram below).

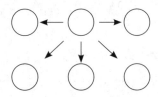

- A space that "blows up" if stepped on *out of order* might become safe when stepped on *in order*.

- It is important to help the person on the board, but wait until they ask for help.

- It works best if helpers speak one at a time.

Play

1. An adult creates a path and diagrams it on a card or tablet that only she can see.

2. The group is helped to come up with an order that they will use to try to get through the minefield. It is usually helpful to line up chairs along one side of the minefield so that the group knows whose turn it is, and that each player has a place to be when it is not his turn in the minefield.

3. The first student steps on to one of the first row of dots.

4. The adult responds by mimicking an explosion, or giving a thumbs-up.

5. The thumbs-up indicates a correct step. That student then gets to take another step.

6. Students leave the minefield if the chosen spot explodes.

7. As the path lengthens, the adult(s) guide the group into ways they can devise to help everyone remember or be coached through the field.

8. When a player makes a misstep on her turn, she is "blown up" and the next person starts into the field.

9. The task is not over until every one in the group has successfully walked the correct path through the minefield.

Many groups like this activity and will ask to repeat it. If a group does it many times and is still interested, the path can be made more difficult by allowing the safe path to double-back and cross over spots more than once.

Goals to use are:

- Pay attention when you are not in the minefield.

- Encourage/help the person in the field (but offer help one at a time).

- Celebrate successes.

- Have fun.

MR. M'S UNO

Uno is a game that most young people have played, and many enjoy. I often use this activity with my younger groups. It is a great activity to use when the group includes individuals who are having difficulty enjoying a game if they are not the winner. I also have added elements designed to help participants learn to transition from great excitement to settling in to focus on play. These are the modifications I make in the rules. I call the game *Mr. M's Uno* as a way to explain to some of my more rigid participants why the rules are slightly different. I let them know that there are clear rules to traditional *Uno*, but that we are playing a variation called *Mr. M's Uno*.

1. Players start with five cards instead of seven.

2. If a player has no play and has to choose from the deck, that player selects only one card. If that card cannot be played, the player says "Pass". (This avoids players becoming either

discouraged by having many, many cards, or having players be unable to organize a large number of cards in order to play.)

3. When someone wins, all players hold on to their cards. That "winner" is designated "first winner", and selects five new cards. The game then continues. The next winner is designated "second winner", and so on. This creates more winners and decreases time spent gathering cards, shuffling, and re-dealing. It also creates multiple opportunities to practice winning and not winning.

4. At the start of the game, the deck is cut until a number is selected. During the game, every time someone plays that number, everyone must jump up and change chairs. This:

    • increases the fun

    • increases the focus on the game when it is not a person's turn

    • leads to excitement as players try to sit next to (or avoid sitting next to) another player

    • allows the leader to reinforce the skill of settling down after a time of great excitement.

Goals for this activity are:

    • Know when it is your turn.

    • Have fun, no matter if you are a winner or not.

    • Laugh a lot.

MOOSE IN THE HOUSE

Moose in the House is a commercially available card game that can be played exactly as designed. This is a great game for working on having fun playing rather than being focused on winning. The adult leaders can influence the outcome of this game by pretending to overreact to having moose played on their "house", thus becoming likely targets for the young players. The young players therefore become more focused on having the adults lose rather than winning themselves, allowing them to work on the skill of enjoying the game no matter the outcome.

Goals for this activity are:

- Know when it is your turn/be ready to play.

- Make sure to give moose cards fairly (adults not included).

- Enjoy the game, no matter how many moose you end up with.

PASSWORD

This is the classic old TV game. It is available commercially, but I do not play by the classic rules. I buy the game in order to get access to many possible words.

I adapt this game by making it into a contest between two teams, with all clues being given by the adult moderator. (You will discover that young people often want to be the person who gives the clues. However, you will also discover that most young people with ASD have a significant delay in thinking about multiple clues. This is one of the reasons that I have adapted the game to have the adult moderator give clues.)

Play

Two teams are established using one of the methods described in the chapters about groups. Co-leaders can be used as either models (and therefore team members) or process-coaches for the teams. A flip of a coin determines which team will get the first clue.

(From that point on, the winning team gets to decide if it wants the first or second clue. One wonderful aspect of this activity is watching the groups slowly come to realize that, in this activity, it is usually better to get the second, fourth, and sixth clues rather than the first, third, and fifth.)

The moderator writes the numbers 10 through 1 vertically on the whiteboard, then gives the first clue, and writes it on the board next to the number ten. The beginning team then discusses their answer. The moderator waits until the team has settled on an answer – it is important not to reward players who call out an answer quickly, even if the answer is correct. An important phrase for the moderator is "Is that your final answer?"

When the team settles on a final answer, the moderator either awards 10 points for being correct, or notes that it is wrong, and writes the answer on the whiteboard next to the clue. The turn then passes to the other team. The moderator gives a second clue, writes it on next to the number nine, and either writes the wrong answer when it is offered, or awards that team nine points. The game continues with declining point values until the word is guessed (or until ten clues have been given).

Begin by selecting the easiest words from the word lists, and move to more difficult words and concepts as the players gain skill.

Suggested goals for this activity are:

- Be "okay" with your teammates.

- Think carefully about all the clues – make one decision.

- Listen to everyone on your team.[2]

PERUDO

Perudo is a commercially available game that is also sold as *Liar's Dice*, and *Pirate Dice*. I play this game with only one variation from the printed directions: when someone has lost a round (and thus lost a die), that individual gets to make the first bet on the subsequent round, but also decides whether the round will go in a clockwise or counter-clockwise direction.

This is a great game for teaching mathematical odds, and also the importance of paying attention to players in order to learn who often plays strictly by the odds, and who might like to bluff and gamble. The rules are a bit complex for beginners to learn. When teaching this game to a whole group, create a poster to explain:

- what "wild die/dice" means

- the two ways that a bet can be raised

- what happens when a player indicates that he "doubts it".

---

2   Often a quiet, non-assertive player catches on to the game and has the correct answer, but louder, more impulsive, players are not listening.

Suggested goals for this game are:

- Pay attention – know what the current "bet" is.

- Watch how other players play, and learn from what you see and hear.

- Have fun, no matter what the result.

I always play along with the group. I'm pretty good at the game and rarely lose many dice. When the first player runs out of dice, I always offer that player my cup so they can continue. Using this model and keeping games to about 20 minutes, rarely is a player forced out of the game by losing all dice. After 20 minutes, the person with the most dice is declared the "first" winner, second most dice is the "second" winner, and so on.

PICK IT

Pick It is a very valuable game that I use extensively in schools groups (late elementary through high school), and adapt so it is played in teams of two players. This game was not commercially available for the last 15 years, so I jealously guarded my two sets. I am pleased to inform all that this game has been reissued by Discovery Toys[3] and is now available (at least in the United States). I have adapted the rules in order to accommodate the learning of teaming skills.

Play

The object of the game is for a team to play one of their cards – by changing the design that is displayed on the table into one of the designs in their hand – by only moving one stick. Designs can be exactly as displayed on the cards, or could be the mirror image of the card, so it is important to explain and demonstrate the concept of mirror image/symmetry.

Divide the group into two-player teams. Shuffle the deck, and deal each team five cards. The cards are to be displayed in front of each team so the teammates can study them, but also so the others

---

3   Go to www.discoverytoys.com in order to find a consultant near you and order this game.

playing the game can see/study them. (This is an important variation from the printed rules of the game.)

The top card of the remaining deck is turned over, and the five sticks are placed into that design. A team is picked to begin play, and the order of play (clockwise or counterclockwise) is determined. Each team studies their cards and determines if they have a move to make. If they do, they make the move and place the card depicting the design they made on the top of the exposed pile of cards. If they think they don't have a move, they must:

1. Ask for help.

2. If no one can help them, they must draw a card from the face down deck. They then can study that card, if they can make that design, they can go ahead and do it.

3. If they can't make that design, the play moves on to the next team.

The game is time-limited. If any team succeeds in using all their cards, they are declared the "first winner", select five cards from the face-down deck, and play goes on. There may be multiple "winners" in this fashion, or, at the end of the time limit, winners may be declared based on the fewest cards.

Note: I have discovered that there are two very difficult cards in the deck. They are the card that depicts the five sticks in a single straight line, and the card that depicts the sticks in a cascade that looks like stairs. I remove these cards when I teach the game to beginners, and only add them in if a very experienced group asks for the challenge of the "tough" cards.

Suggested goals:

• Be "okay" with your teammate.

• Work together with your teammate.

• Wait to help until asked.[4]

---

4   This is extremely important. The fun of this game is teammates figuring out the puzzle themselves. Other players learn to respect this opportunity for others by restraining themselves when they can see a move, but the other team cannot.

PIT

Pit is also readily commercially available. The only rule modification I make is to ignore the point values on the cards and simply play until one person has obtained all the commodities in a chosen category. I only play this game with community groups, and never set goals. We just play for fun.

QUESTION CARDS

This activity builds on the skills that were worked on during the opening introductory activity. As a matter of fact, the three goals for this game are exactly the same:

- Wait for your turn to speak.

- Listen with your eyes and your ears.

- Make sure every opinion/answer is treated as "okay".

The activity differs in the following ways:

1. No longer will everyone answer the same question. Each person gets to select his question.

2. The questions are found on cards contained in *The Question* box.[5]

3. Group members are told that, if they hear/see a question that they wished to answer, not to worry. All they have to do is tell the leader they are interested in that question, and the leader puts that card on display on the chalk ledge of the whiteboard. When it is an individual's turn, he can either select from the top of the shuffled cards, or select one of the cards on display.

4. This means only the person who goes first has to select a random card. The leader finds out who is interested in going first, and comes up with a fair way to pick the first person if more than one wants to go first.

---

5   *The Question* box is available at www.superduperinc.com/products. Type "The Question" in search box. *The Question* contains about 200 questions – out of which I have selected 25 to use. However, the cards are colorful, the type is large, and they are very durable. I found the investment in the box to be worth the money.

5. A decision is made about going clockwise or counterclockwise, and the activity continues until each participant has had the same number of turns.

6. The group then evaluates using the above goals.

SMART ASS

Smart Ass is commercially available, and I use it with community groups. The name gets a measure of shocked reaction from both players and parents, but the game is about knowledge – and everyone has learned to get past the name.

I play the game in my community groups with very little variation from the printed rules. I rotate the responsibility of giving the clues either clockwise or counterclockwise so that everyone experiences being the "host" of the game show. I also reinforce calling on participants to give an answer after each clue based on the order that hands are raised. It is very hard for most of my participants to notice and keep track of when players raise their hands, so I always take on this responsibility. Once a question is asked, I point to the players in the order that I have observed the raising of the hands.

The only other variation I make is allowing players to "pass" on the *Who* cards. There are *Who, What* and *Where* cards, and I have discovered that most of my young people can answer the *What* and *Where* cards, but many cannot identify the people being described on the *Who* cards. We have developed a simple rule. A player who rolls the die and is directed to take a *Who* card selects up to three cards. If she does not know any of the three persons selected, that player can decide to take a *What* or *Where* card.

I have never used *Smart Ass* at a school – I don't want to have to deal with parents or staff members who are upset about the name of the game.

Three goals that could be used with this activity are:

- Listen to, and remember, the clues and what has already been guessed.

- Play fair – call on players in the order in which they have raised hands.

- Congratulate the player who is correct – and is thus that round's *Smart Ass*.

SORT IT OUT

Sort it Out is another great two-team game that promotes a group of players making decisions together. Basically, it provides lists of five items in a category, and asks players to sort the items in various ways – shortest to tallest, lightest to heaviest, youngest to oldest, and so on. Once again, I have adapted the rules to promote the skills I am seeking to develop. I do not use the game board, but divide the players into two teams.

Play

The teams are placed on two sides of the room. Read the way the items are to be sorted, and give the teams the five items. At the same time, write the list on the whiteboard.

While the teams are deliberating, create a grid next to the lists so that as teams respond, numbers can be written in the grid indicating the order that has been decided upon. In order to make sure a team does not learn from the other team's list, solicit the order in this fashion:

- Ask Team 1 for its first item in the list.
- Next, ask Team 2 for its first and second items.
- Next, Team 1 gives its second and third items.
- Team 2 gives items three and four.
- Team 1 gives items four and five.
- Team 2 gives item five.

Compare the lists and decide together which team got closest to the actual order. Then move on to a new question.

Suggested goals are:

- Listen to each other – decide together.

- If there is difficulty reaching agreement, find a way to compromise.

- Laugh a lot.

TSURO

Tsuro is a board game that is currently not in production. I include it here in case you own it or can get it from a friend or relative, second-hand or online.

This is a game in which up to eight players end up constructing a maze made of tiles through which their designated stones must move. The more tiles added, the harder it is to find a safe path.

I do not use this game in any school group, or in beginning community groups. I use this in community groups once the culture has been established. It is terrific for working on conversation skills while also playing a game. The game is not so difficult that players need to be intensely focused when it is not their turn, and, when a player is taking a turn, it does not require such intense concentration that players will be asking the others to be quiet. Thus it is a great game to work on multitasking – which is undeniably an employment skill. If you can find it – get it. Then enjoy it.

TURNABOUT

Think *Uno* on steroids. This commercial game is much more complex than *Uno*. I use it in my community groups as a way to help the teens move from the simplicity of *Uno* to a more complex game that will challenge any peers that might be asked to play.

TWENTY QUESTIONS

I adapt *Twenty Questions* in a manner similar to the way I do *Password* in order to use it to focus on the skill of small groups working to reach consensus.

Two teams are created, and a co-leader is placed on the least skilled team or assigned to be a "coach" to both teams.

The other leader acts as the "host" of the game who will give all the clues.

The first information the host gives is whether the two teams will be trying to identify a *person, place,* or *thing.* Once that is established, one team gets to ask the first question. All questions have to be asked in a manner that will allow the host to answer either "Yes" or "No".

As the questions are asked and answered, the host writes the questions and answers on the whiteboard. The host and co-leader then assist the groups with the posted information in creating questions that will allow them to home in on the possible answers. They also help the teams figure out what to do when team members disagree about what to ask next. Thus the skills of listening to each other and compromising are also reinforced.

This is a great game for school and community groups.

Suggested goals are:

- Listen to each other/make decisions together.

- Think about the information on the whiteboard.

- Have fun, regardless of the results.

UP THE RIVER

This is a fabulous game to use for school and community groups in order to promote the skills needed to work with a partner. It has not been produced or sold for about 20 years.

Fortunately, the owner of the copyright, Ravensburger[6], has given me permission to reproduce the game board and rules here. I am very appreciative. I use this game more than any other activity. Young people ages eight through 14 seem to really enjoy it. Here is what you need.

Copy out the game board that follows this description. I like to let some of the young people color the board. Cut the river pieces (numbered 1 through 10) into separate strips. Then attach them to cardboard and either laminate the pieces or cover them with clear mailing tape.

---

6   Ravensburger, of course, holds this copyright. Reproduction of this game in order to sell it is prohibited.

The object of the game is to sail boats up the river and into the dock. The first boat gets to "dock" on the number 12 post and gets 12 points, the second on 11, etc. The object of the game is to get the most points. Boats can enter the dock without having the exact number to do so.

Use a six-sided dice. Put a sticker over the six. This is now "Good wind/Bad wind". (See special rules below.)

1. The dock is at the top of the river. River cards are lined up with card #10 at the top and #1 at the bottom.

2. Each team gets three boats. All boats begin their voyage on card #4.

3. Upon each roll, a team can only move one boat – no splitting a move between two boats.

4. After all teams have had a turn, the river flows: the bottom card comes to the top and everything slides back. Each time the teams have all completed a turn, the bottom card comes forwards ("the river flows").

5. Any boat that is on the bottom card when it comes forwards "sinks" and is out of the game.

Special rules

- If you can land on the tide (card #5) on your turn, you go ahead three more cards.

- All teams must stop on the sandbar (card #1) – even if they have rolled a number that would normally put them beyond the sandbar. However, remember, you can't get off the sandbar (and thus into the dock) until you are on the sandbar.

- Good wind/bad wind – When you roll Good Wind/Bad wind, one of three things happen.

   1. Your team can move one of your boats up to your *next closest* boat. (You cannot skip over one of your boats. You can, however, skip over the sandbar.)

2. Your team can send an opponent's boat back to their *next closest* boat.

3. If you only have one boat, or if all your boats are on the same card, your team can reroll so that you have a chance to move forwards.

Important: these rules only apply to boats on the river. You cannot move one of your boats into the dock, or move an opponent's boat out of the dock. Good wind/Bad wind comes into play on the second round. If any team rolls Good wind/Bad wind on their first roll, they simply roll again.

If time runs out before all boats dock, boats are brought into the dock in the order they appear on the river in order to determine first winner, second winner, and so on. If boats are tied on the same card, the leader shakes those boats in his hand in order to mix them, and then drops them one by one. The first boat dropped gets the higher number on the dock, etc.

Suggested goals are:

• Be "okay" with you teammate.

• Teammates make decisions together.

• Have fun no matter if you are first winner, second winner, third winner, or fourth winner.

Up the River – Dock posts

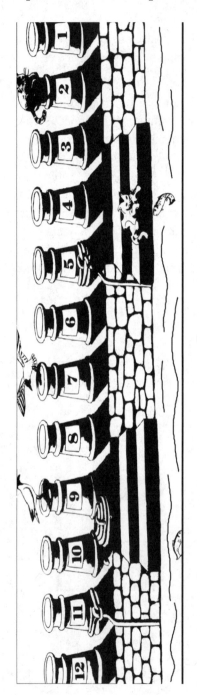

Up the River – Strips 6–10

Up the River – Strips 1–5

Index

Note: The abbreviation ASD is used for autism spectrum disorder.

A Through Z Game 178–9
Apples to Apples 179–80
Ask for Help 170–1
Ask to Play 164–8
Ask to Share 172–3
Asperger's syndrome 11, 12, 21
  see also Karl's story
associative thinking
  application of logical thought 63–4
  benefits of 61–2
  lack of understanding in school 61, 64
  word association game 60
attention challenges
  activities while waiting to begin 42–3
  attention-shifting 44–5
  establishing joint attention 43–4
  manipulatives 44
  most common 42
Autism Advocate 20
Autism Society of Minnesota
  annual conference 14–15, 80

band of regulation 27
  adult's wide band 28
  ASD-affected person's band 29–30
  children's narrow band 29
  Guiding Toward Growth interventions 30–1
  visual representation 27
Bean Bag Toss 122, 176–7, 180
behavior issues 18–19, 72–4
  see also straight line behavior

Big Dice 79, 161–4
bike-riding 70
blaming adults 49–50
block schedules 40–1
Bocce Ball 180–1
brain development 23–4

card games *see* table games
Challenger Division, Little League baseball program 130, 146
challenges to teaching social enjoyment 35–6
  associative thinking 60–4
  attention 42–5
  emotional regulation 46–50
  language processing 55–9
  motivational deficits 82–5
  organization 51–4
  routine 37–41
  sensory sensitivities 65–71
  stereotyping 77–81
  "unlearning" rituals 72–6
Charades 169
chess analogy 82–3
co-leadership 91–2
  see also leaders
Commonyms 43, 141
community-based groups 42
  discussion strategies 149–52
  extended activities 130–1, 146
  fun time 152
  "gathering" strategies 141–2
  goals 135–6, 137, 138
  leaders 94–5
  locations 129–30, 149–50
  non-stimulating environment 96
  open-ended 127–9

overviews for specific age groups 132–3, 139–40, 148–9
  parents, meetings between 130, 147
  peer group members 97
  planning 142
  preparation for 91–2, 129
  qualities and compliments 145–6, 152
  repetition, use of 98
  rewards 138
  schedules 95
  skills development delay 133–4
  small groups, need for 134–5
  space for 92–4
  structure 135–6
  switching activities 144
  whole-group activities 144–5
compliments, use of 104–6, 117, 145–6, 152
consistency
  of group leaders 94–5
  of group schedules 95
  of group space 92–3
conversation activities
  A Through Z Game 178–9
  Evaluation Process 117–19
  goals for 113–15, 135
  Introductory Questions 184–5
  Loaded Questions 186–7
  Question Cards 195–6
  Tsuro 198

Depot Coffee House (Minneapolis) 128, 149–50
developmental delay 23–6
directions, understanding 58–9

Discovery Toys 193
discussion
    strategies for 149–52
    talking at length 60, 114
    see also conversation
        activities
Dominion 181

eating issues 67
echolalia 59
Einstein, Albert 61
emotional/behavior disability
    (E/BD) 18
emotional regulation
    David's story 49–50
    delays in developing
        emotional control
        46–8
    Social Stories technique
        48–9
employment 12–13, 21
    statistics 20
environment
    non-stimulating 95–6
    safe 94
evaluation 117–19, 123
Evaluation Process 117–19
expressive language 56–8,
    110

First/Last Game 181–2
Fosbury, Dick 62
Frisbee Golf 182
FunJoyment groups 89–90
    origins 11–17
    see also community-based
        groups; school-based
        groups

game activities
    Bean Bag Toss 122, 176–7,
        180
    Mr. M's Minefield 187–9
    Pick It 116, 122, 193–4
    Up The River 122,
        199–204
goals
    by activity 115–17, 135–6
    daily 113–15, 122–3
    for games 137
    reaching 119–20, 123–4,
        138
golf analogy 21–2
group process 165–7

Guiding Toward Growth
    program 20, 26, 30–1
    origins 11–17
Gutstein, Steven 14–15

hearing 66–7
help, asking for 137
    see also Ask for Help
hinting (as skill to be learned)
    163–4
"horizon problem" 20
hosts, of games 124–5
hurdles *see* challenges
    to teaching social
        enjoyment

ignore/observe technique
    72–3
illness, recognition of 71
Imaginiff 183
In a Pickle 183–4
Individual Education Plan
    (IEP) 14
individuals, games for
    Apples to Apples 179–80
    Imaginiff 183
    Kinder Bunnies 186
    Moose in the House 190–1
    Mr. M's Uno 189–90
    Smart Ass 196–7
information processing 58–9
intelligence 82–3
Interrupting an Adult 174–5
interventions
    nature of effective 36
    reasons for 30–1
Introductory Questions 184–5

jewels
    counting 110–11
    use of 101–3, 108–9, 110,
        165–6

Karl's story 18–19
keeping things the same *see*
    routine
Kenny, Sister, Elizabeth 61–2
Kids on Stage 169
Killer Bunnies 185
Kinder Bunnies 186

language processing
    expressive language 56–8,
        110
    Kent's story 56–8

receptive language 58–9
    ritualized language 59
    speech professionals 13, 55
leaders
    as game hosts 124–5
    need for consistency 94–5
    number required 99, 112,
        121, 132, 139, 148
learning steps 25–6
Liar's Dice 192
listening skills 114
listening skills games
    Apples to Apples 179–80
    Imaginiff 183
    Introductory Questions
        184–5
    Twenty Questions 198–9
Little League baseball
    program, Challenger
    Division 130, 146
Loaded Questions 186–7
locations for groups 129–30,
    149–50

manipulatives 44
Marshall, Barry J. 62
"meltdown" 39–40
Merges, Kelly 16–17, 130–1,
    146
Moose in the House 190–1
motivation
    Billy's story 84–5
    chess analogy 82–3
    role of praise 85, 109–10
Mr. M's Minefield 187–9
Mr. M's Uno 189–90

neurotypical individuals
    learning and development
        47, 133–4
    as peer group members
        96–7, 103
    stereotyping by 77–81
Nobel Prize in Physiology or
    Medicine (2005) 62
noise, difficulty in processing
    66–7

open-ended groups 127–9
organization
    difficulties in learning 54
    Jacki's story 52–3
    Rick's story 53–4
    as a skill 51

outdoor games
  Bocce Ball 180–1
  Frisbee Golf 182

parents
  meetings between 130,
    147
  restoring control 77–8
  role in teaching skills 41
Password 191–2
peer group members
  in community-based
    groups 97
  in school-based groups
    96–7
permission letters 155
  general 156
  seeking negative reply 157
  seeking positive reply 158
  when starting a group 159
Perudo 192–3
Piaget, Jean 23
Pick It 116, 122, 193–4
Pirate Dice 192
Pit 195
posters, use of 100–1
  examples 168, 171, 173,
    175
"power-readers" 78
praise, role of 85, 109–10
Pratt, Cathy 20
preparation for groups 91–2,
  129
proprioception 69–71
puzzles 43, 141

qualities 145–6, 152
  see also compliments, use of
Question Cards 195–6

Ravensburger 199
receptive language 58–9
regulation see band of
    regulation; emotional
    regulation
Relationship Development
  Intervention (RDI)
  14–15
repetition, use of
  in community-based
    groups 98
  in school-based groups 98
rewards, use of 73–4,
  119–20, 123–4, 138
  see also jewels

ritualized language 59
rituals 13–14
  Clint's story 74–6
  ignore/observe technique
    72–3
  Ready to start 102–4
  rewards process 73–4
  see also routine
Roberts Apperception Test for
  Children cards 84
role-play games
  Ask for Help 170–1
  Ask to Play 164–8
  Ask to Share 172–3
  Interrupting an Adult 174–5
routine
  as emotional security
    blanket 39–40
  loss of, causing "meltdown"
    38–9
  parental role 41
  reactions to loss of 37–8
  Social Stories technique 39
  use of block schedule 40–1
  see also rituals

safe environment 94
schedules
  block 40–1
  consistency of 95
  of groups 133, 140, 149
  whiteboard for visual 101
school-based groups
  compliments, giving and
    receiving 104–6, 117
  evaluation 117–19, 123
  game hosts 124–5
  goals 113–15, 115–17,
    119–20, 122–3,
    123–4
  jewels 101–3, 108–9,
    110–11, 165–6
  leaders 94–5
  non-stimulating
    environment 95–6
  overviews for specific age
    groups 99, 112, 121
  peer group members 97–8
  praising oneself 109–10
  preparation for 91–2
  Ready to start ritual 102–4
  repetition, use of 98
  rewards 119–20, 123–4

scoreboard, use of 101–2,
  160
space for 92–4
straight line behavior
  107–9
two-team games 124–6
whiteboard, use of 100–1,
  113–14, 122
scoreboard, use of 101–2,
  160
Scott's story 15–16
sensory sensitivities 65–71
  see also proprioception;
    senses, e.g. smell,
    vision; "whole body
    feel"
sight, sense of 65–6
Sister Kenny Institute
  (Minneapolis) 61–2
Smart Ass 196–7
smell, sense of 68
social enjoyment, as skill that
  can be learned 21–4
  see also challenges to
    teaching social
    enjoyment
social interaction see social
    enjoyment
Social Stories 39, 48–9
Sort It Out 197–8
sounds, difficulty in
  processing 66–7
space, for groups
  consistency 92–3
  dedication of 93
  safe 94
speech professionals 13, 55
steps, learning 25–6
stereotyping assumptions
  of cleverness 78
  of cognitive impairment 79
  of lack of interest 79–80
  of stubbornness 77–8
  of "weirdness" 80–1
straight line behavior 107–9

table games
  Dominion 181
  In a Pickle 183–4
  Killer Bunnies 185
  Moose in the House 190–1
  Mr. M's Uno 189–90
  Perudo 192–3
  Pick It 116, 122, 193–4

table games *continued*
   Pit 195
   Question Cards 195–6
   Tsuro 198
   Turnabout 198
taste, sense of 67
team games *see* two-team
   games
teamwork 115–17
touch, sense of 68–9
transition programs 16, 74–6
Tsuro 198
Turnabout 198
Twenty Questions 198–9
Twister mats 187
two-team games 124–5
   Bean Bag Toss 122, 176–7,
      180
   Bocce Ball 180–1
   Loaded Questions 186–7
   Password 191–2
   Sort It Out 197–8
   Twenty Questions 198–9

Up The River 122, 199–204
"upside down" therapy 46

videotapes 13–14, 19
vision, sense of 65–6

Warren, Robin 62
whiteboard, use of 45, 59,
      100–1, 113–14, 122,
      135, 145
"whole body feel" 71
whole-group activities 144–5
   Apples to Apples 179–80
   Imaginiff 183
   Loaded Questions 186–7
   Smart Ass 196–7
   Sort It Out 197–8
   Twenty Questions 198–9
Wii games 138, 142–3, 152
word association game 60
Wright brothers 63
Wuzzles 43, 141